It has been two
hundred years since the
birth of the United States
Constitution. Countless
Americans have courageously
defended its freedoms
since then. May you and
I stand firm together in
our resolve to always
hold high the "light of
liberty".

Paul H. Dunn

THE LIGHT OF LIBERTY

PAUL H. DUNN

Bookcraft
Salt Lake City, Utah

Library of Congress Catalog Card Number: 87-70858
ISBN 0-88494-629-0

First Printing, 1987

Printed in the United States of America

CONTENTS

PREFACE

Years of reflection on battles experienced as a young man during World War II have stirred within me a desire to share feelings concerning liberty. All too often in the mechanics of daily living, we forget to ponder and consider our great heritage and the price that was paid for freedom.

It seems only appropriate that during the celebration of the bicentennial of our Constitution that I express my love and appreciation for America and what it means to me.

As always, it should be stated that this book is not an official publication of the Church and the author alone is responsible for its contents.

As in times past I express gratitude to many who have made this publication possible. To Sharene Hansen and Elaine Seaman, able secretaries who have done their share to bring this project to completion. A special thanks to David Christensen for ideas and suggestions. Most of all I express my appreciation to my wife, Jeanne, whose care and attention to editing and detail permit me to express feelings and ideas in ways that alone I could not.

And finally I express my great debt and gratitude to the many patriots, past and present, who have made America such a blessed land; with a hope and prayer that my children and their children will continue to understand the principles that made her great and will dedicate their lives to its preservation.

PROLOGUE

It seems ironic that, as an eleventh-grade student at Hollywood High School in California, I was asked by my history teacher to prepare a report of a current event to give before the class. My subject was the fall of Bataan and Corregidor in December of 1941. Little did I realize as I stood before my class reporting General Douglas MacArthur's now-famous promise to the Philippine people, "I shall return," that I would be in the infantry assault wave on the island of Leyte on an October morning in 1944, two days ahead of MacArthur's return.

Many years later, in General Douglas MacArthur's final address to the Corps of Cadets at West Point, he asked these would-be soldiers to remember throughout their careers and lives their motto of *Duty, Honor, Country,* which motto he and his comrades of three wars had held to while "bending under soggy packs, on many a weary march from dripping dusk to drizzling dawn, slogging ankle deep through the mire of shell-shocked roads, to form grimly for the attack, blue-lipped, covered with sludge and mud, chilled by the wind and rain, driving home to their objective." He recalled "the filth of murky foxholes, the stench of ghostly trenches, the slime of dripping dugouts; those broiling suns of relentless heat, those torrential rains of devastating storm, the loneliness and utter desolation of jungle trails, the bitterness of long separation from those they loved and cherished, and deadly pestilence of tropical disease, the horror of stricken areas of war;

their resolute and determined defense, their swift and sure attack, their indomitable purpose, their complete and decisive victory—always victory—always through the bloody haze of their last reverberating shot, the vision of gaunt, ghastly men reverently following [the] password of Duty—Honor—Country."

He concluded by saying that "the soldier, above all other people, prays for peace, for he must suffer and bear the deepest wounds and scars of war." (Douglas MacArthur, *Reminiscences* [New York: McGraw-Hill Book Co., 1964], pp. 424, 426.)

To the thousands of patriots in our history who have known war firsthand and have experienced the price of liberty and peace, and to the tens of thousand others like them who have followed, we, the current and future generations, owe tremendous gratitude and a continuing remembrance of the courage, devotion, and sacrifice that made America great.

I shall never forget the feelings I had as a young soldier when time after time I was called upon to place in shallow temporary graves the lifeless bodies of my comrades in arms, some unknown to me, many others with whom I had trained and to whom I had grown close. I couldn't help but remember their wishes and desires for the future.

On an island far away in the Pacific our regiment placed the following inscription above the entrance of a temporary cemetery:

We Gave Our Todays
In Order That You Might Have Your Tomorrows

May God grant us the vision, understanding, and determination to make those tomorrows worthy of the sacrifices of our hero dead, and may the world never forget that all future wars and conflicts will again and always cost the lives of the elite of our nations, in order to keep the "light of liberty."

PART I

FOUNDATIONS

LIFE AND LIBERTY

" *If we truly cherish the heritage we have received, we must maintain the same virtues and . . . character of our stalwart forebears—faith in God, courage, industry, frugality, self-reliance, and integrity. We have the obligation to maintain what those who pledged their lives, their fortunes, and their sacred honor gave to future generations. . . .*

. . . I thank God for the sacrifices and efforts made by our Founding Fathers, whose efforts brought us the blessings we have today. Their lives should be reminders to us that we are blessed beneficiaries of a liberty earned by great sacrifice of property, reputation, and life. **"**

EZRA TAFT BENSON

CHAPTER 1

"OH, BEAUTIFUL FOR PATRIOT DREAM"

Some years ago in the summer heat of Boston, two men worked vigorously and perspired mightily to construct displays for the American Bicentennial. One stopped to mop his brow and asked the other, "Do we really have to go through this every two hundred years?" The correct answer of course, is that we have not celebrated often or deeply enough the birth of this promised land, this choice and beautiful and still-young land, which we possess as the Lord's gift in freedom and joy—just as long as we serve Him.

Boston is a proper place to begin; Boston, in fact, is "a very proper place." We who have prayed, preached, and tracted in lovely New England found it, though proper, not all that formal. It is a charming place with friendly, wonderful people. On all sides you see the "where it happened" of precious American tradition.

Indeed, it has been just over two hundred years since a better-than-average silversmith on a black horse made history, as Longfellow later recalled:

The fate of a nation was riding that night;
And the spark struck out by that steed in his
    flight . . .
A cry of defiance, and not of fear . . .
And the midnight message of Paul Revere.

That's the way it was from Boston to Lexington to Concord as the war for independence and liberty began. Most of all, it was for people—men and women of courage and vision and faith, strengthened by God as part of His plan; people who struggled, froze, starved, and when necessary, died so that these free states in union might be born, in Thomas Jefferson's incisive words, "to assume, among the powers of the earth, the separate and equal station to which the laws of nature and of nature's God entitle them" (Declaration of Independence).

It was worth a lot to the new Americans of that hour to give life to this nation—worth all they had, all they were, and all that they had dreamed. What is it worth today to you and to me and especially to us as Latter-day Saints, who alone know what the Lord is doing to assert our free agency toward the fulfilling of His plan?

As you decide, let me suggest an exciting tour for you. Go, if you can—and if you cannot, then make the trip in your mind's eye from your study or your armchair or your library, but go—go to Charlestown and

Breed's Hill; to Washington's Crossing, Brandywine Creek, Saratoga; to the great courthouse and a dozen more; to King's Mountain and Cowpens and Guilford Courthouse on the road to Yorktown where it finally ended. Ask yourself along the way who these people were and where they got their vision; listen intently for a drummer boy tapping out a song that is two centuries older than George M. Cohan.

Give a thought as well to a lad aged twenty-one who regretted that he had but one life to give for his country and to a twenty-year-old French major general who came three thousand miles to secure the final victory. And if you are traveling and you come to one of those too-numerous claims that "George Washington slept here," and you kind of hope that, if so, the sheets have been changed and that modern plumbing has been installed, pause to remember that there really was such a man as George Washington—sometimes disliked, but respected, gladly followed, and superbly there when we needed him most to lead in carrying out the plan of the Lord in the founding of America. Childless, the Virginia planter today has 250 million living children. You and I are among them. God had set him apart and lifted him up.

Carry on with me then to Philadelphia to the year 1787. Gathered to frame a constitution in cramped and overheated quarters, delegates from most of the thirteen sovereign states struggled through the summer months to produce a document upon which a free nation might be built. Fortunately (and it has been said by those not of our faith), they achieved a constitution and a bill of rights which far exceeded the best that could come from these men. But it did more than that.

It was and is a living document capable of defending its basic principles but flexible enough to adapt to the needs of this changing and growing United States.

You and I are made aware, of course, that there is a better explanation of what really occurred. The scriptures tell us, "And for this purpose have I established the Constitution of this land, by the hands of wise men whom I raised up unto this very purpose, and redeemed the land by the shedding of blood" (D&C 101:80).

The land was "redeemed," indeed, by thousands killed and wounded along the way at Germantown, at Bemis Heights, at Charlestown, and at so many other places in the American Revolution.

President Brigham Young spoke for himself and for every living prophet who has since addressed the question when he said, "The signers of the Declaration of Independence and the framers of the Constitution were inspired from on high to do that work" (*Journal of Discourses* 7:14).

An objective study of the delegates involved—their fears, their limitations, their vested interests, and their lives—makes it clear that they were not the sort of men we usually think of as prophets. Nonetheless, they were inspired, and the Constitution they provided can be designated accurately as a divine document.

But even a divine constitution requires something further; it demands a kind of people who will, by their very natures, receive and respect such a constitution and function well within the conditions it establishes.

Again the Lord said: "Wherefore, this land is consecrated unto him whom he shall bring. And if it so be that they shall serve him according to the commandments which he hath given, it shall be a land of liberty unto them." (2 Nephi 1:7.)

As Latter-day Saints then, we know why some persons came to America and others did not. And as someone has said, "We haven't done badly for a nation of immigrants." We are immigrants, you and I, because the Lord made immigrants of us and brought us here. We have done as well as could be expected and are richly blessed despite our shortcomings because the Lord has thus far held us in His hands and worked His purposes, including His ultimate purpose, through us.

Can you understand that this is what America is all about? You and I know, and you and I *alone* really know, the reason for this blessed and beautiful land. In a world where men have given up on this most vital question, we know the purpose of America.

This country did not end in Philadelphia, even if Horace Greeley did mean that city when he urged us to "go west." It was a new land, fresh, clean, unspoiled by a past. America included the frontier. In 1805 the Prophet Joseph Smith was born, and he grew up toward adolescence just like the new land. He fitted it. He was young, clean, unspoiled—an innocent young lad without a past, kneeling in a quiet grove in a pristine land—and the Lord reached out and kept His promise. He established His conditions over centuries; you see, God has time. His plan made it possible for the holy priesthood and the Church to be restored upon the earth—the restoration of the gospel of Jesus Christ —but only in America.

Can you understand the way God has worked? And if you do, will you join me this day in committing yourself to preach the message of the Lord's glorious achievement in America and to teach it as messengers wherever the opportunity allows? This is a time when you and I can afford to be patriotic in the best sense of that term. There is reason to be proud that we live in an established land that has been conditioned by the Lord so that His gospel could be restored. The purpose of America was to provide a setting wherein that was possible. All else in this country's history takes its power from that one great, central purpose.

As some of you may know, I have never counted mathematics as my most exciting subject. Nevertheless, I believe that I can set in sequence the steps the Lord has used in His plan.

First, there was selecting and bringing the people here. The next step was establishing a free nation. The third was inspiring a divine constitution. The fourth was opening the American frontier—new land, fresh and clean. The fifth step was calling young Joseph Smith to become a prophet in such a little time—God's prophet, seer, and revelator, and later His martyr.

Let me add one final stop to your American journey. The place: Arlington National Cemetery in Arlington, Virginia—the tomb of America's unknown soldier. Today the remains of three servicemen from three wars lie there. The inscription reminds us, "Here rests in honored glory an American soldier known but to God." There are in addition some five thousand other unknown servicemen buried in Arlington; and all across the nation and the world I have seen the crosses, row upon row, marking the places where lie America's honored dead, literally in the thousands. What did it cost them so that this nation might remain "the land of liberty?" How shall we honor them, you and I?

We can do so in two ways, it seems to me: first, by striving to make our citizenry the righteous people the Lord requires of us; second, by telling the story of what the Lord has done for you and me and this great church and why.

> Oh, beautiful for patriot dream
> That sees beyond the years
> Thine alabaster cities gleam,
> Undimmed by human tears!
> America! America!
> God shed his grace on thee,
> And crown thy good with brotherhood
> From sea to shining sea.
> (Katherine Bates, "America the Beautiful,"
> *Hymns,* no. 338.)

May that be the song of our hearts and our prayers for fulfillment.

" We are rearing a generation that does not seem to understand the fundamentals of our American way of life, a generation that is no longer dedicated to its preservation. . . . We can only appreciate freedom if we understand the comparative fruits thereof. "

EZRA TAFT BENSON

" As Americans, we cannot but believe that our political creed goes down in its foundations to the solid rock of truth. . . . Thus the duty rests today, more heavily than ever, upon each American citizen to make good to the world those principles upon which this government was built. "

WINSTON CHURCHILL

CHAPTER 2

"I PLEDGE ALLEGIANCE"

"I pledge allegiance to the flag
of the United States of America and
to the Republic for which it stands,
one nation under God,
indivisible, with liberty and
justice for all."

As Americans, both you and I have stood with thousands of others and repeated the Pledge of Allegiance. I suppose I have done that same thing hundreds of times in the past. Each time I do, a special feeling comes over me as I place my hand on my heart and face the flag.

As I have pondered the material for this book, I have considered seriously the implications of what allegiance is all about. We use the term so easily, so lightly, and yet I have a feeling that perhaps this is wrong.

Almost everyone who knows me knows I love stories. I love to hear them and tell them. In my opinion, stories teach just about as well as anything can. Many good friends constantly send me copies of stories they find. As I was considering the principle of allegiance, I read a great story given me by such a friend. It concerns a major in the United States Air Force. Most important, it concerns allegiance and what that may require—at least of some. Here's the story in Major Maxwell's own words:

"We were over the Texas panhandle at 34,000 feet. Just before 11:00 P.M., April 28, the number six engine of our Strategic Air Command jet bomber exploded and engulfed the right wing in flames. The order was given, 'Bail out.'

"The pilots blew off the canopy to clear their ejection track upward into the night.

"That's all I remember of this phase of the ordeal: the canopy decompression blast tore my helmet loose, slammed me against a bulkhead and knocked me unconscious. I lay in the darkness, my chutepack gone, my oxygen mask ripped from my face, my life draining away.

"What followed appears miraculous: the ejection seat of Lieutenant James E. Obenauf failed to fire. He tried to bail out of the entrance hatch, but it jammed. As he started forward to the navigator's ejection hatch, he stumbled over me in the dark passageway.

"The plane was on fire and seemed about to break up. But Lieutenant Obenauf did not jump. He climbed back into his dangerously hot ejection seat and with all the skill and prayer he could muster flew the seemingly doomed ninety-ton, six-engine jet single-handed.

During his rapid descent to save me, and all the way home, a terrific wind tore at his face unmercifully. Almost an hour later, when he arrived over Dyess Air Force Base, he was nearly blind. And yet, descending through heavy clouds and turbulance, he managed an 'impossible' one-man landing. The man who might have simply jumped and saved himself had brought me back from the dead.

"The next morning, the sun poured down with a special warmth. I had a fresh viewpoint on everything around me. I realized I had been given what many people wish for: a second chance at life.

"The pressures and problems of everyday life seem easy for me now.

"To Jim Obenauf I'll be forever grateful. His courageous action makes it possible for me to guide my six children through their important formative years. I feel that his decision was primarily a reflection of the way he grew up, the character of his way of life. And that will remain always an inspiration for me and my children." *(This Week.)*

Major Maxwell's allegiance to his fellowmen is typical of my own experience in time of war. Allegiance to people and to this country sometimes requires great sacrifice. It may cost more than we imagine. I have seen young men "pledge their allegiance" with their lives.

As I have considered Major Maxwell's story and my own experiences, I have wondered if perhaps the time may come when we will all be required to "pledge our allegiance" with more than our words. I have a feeling that such acts are those which have made our country great.

A review of the beginnings of this great nation confirms the fact that allegiance can be costly. The fifty-six signers of the Declaration of Independence are a perfect example of what it means to pledge allegiance to this flag of ours:

"Five signers were captured by the British as traitors, and tortured before they died. Twelve had their homes ransacked and burned. Two lost their sons in the Revolutionary Army; another had two sons captured. Nine of the fifty-six fought and died from wounds or the hardship of the Revolutionary War.

"What kind of men were they? Twenty-four were lawyers and jurists. Eleven were merchants, nine were farmers and large plantation owners, men of means and well educated. But they signed the Declaration of Independence knowing full well that the penalty would be death if they were captured.

"Carter Braxton of Virginia, a wealthy planter and trader, saw his ships swept from the seas by the British navy. He sold his home and properties to pay his debts, and died in rags.

"Thomas McKean was so hounded by the British that he was forced to move his family almost constantly. He served in Congress without pay, and his family was kept in hiding. His possessions were taken from him, and poverty was his reward.

"Vandals or soldiers or both looted the properties of Ellery, Clymer, Hall, Walton, Gwinnett, Heyward, Rutledge, and Middleton. Francis Lewis had his home and properties destroyed. The enemy jailed his wife and she died within a few months.

"At the Battle of Yorktown, Thomas Nelson, Jr., noted that the British General Cornwallis had taken over the Nelson home for his headquarters. The owner quietly urged General George Washington to open fire, which was done. The home was destroyed, and Nelson died bankrupt.

"John Hart was driven from his wife's bedside as she was dying. Their thirteen children fled for their lives. His fields and grist mill were laid waste. For more than a year he lived in forests and caves, returning home after the war to find his wife dead, his children vanished. A few weeks later he died from exhaustion and a broken heart. Morris and Livingston suffered similar fates."

Such were the stories and sacrifices of the American Revolution. These were not wild-eyed, rabble-rousing ruffians; they were soft-spoken men of means and education. They had security, but they valued liberty more.

Although there was no official "Pledge of Allegiance" for these great patriots, they put into words their own pledge. Their statement of allegiance has been memorized and quoted ever since. Here are those memorable words:

"For the support of this declaration, with a firm reliance on the protection of the Divine Providence, we mutually pledge to each other, our lives, our fortunes, and our sacred honor."

And they meant it! Somehow I can't believe that those fifty-six Americans all expected to pay the price they did. But the fact that they were willing to do so is remarkable.

Since the time of our founding fathers, men and women have continued to pledge their lives, their fortunes, and their sacred honor.

Abraham Lincoln pledged his all for our country and he gave it. But even before his assassination, he knew what it meant to give—and not to be appreciated. I smile every time I read the story of his spirited battle with Steven Douglas for a seat in the Senate. After his defeat, Lincoln remarked that he felt like the boy who had stubbed his toe: "It hurt too bad to laugh, and he was too big to cry."

Giving our lives, our fortunes, and our honor are not always noted. Nevertheless, since Lincoln's time, hundreds of thousands of valiant Americans have continued to do so. Thousands upon thousands did so in World War I. They continued to do so in World War II, in Korea, in Vietnam, in Lebanon, throughout all the world. While there are some—such as President John F. Kennedy and his brother Robert, together with Martin Luther King and others—who have been recognized for their ultimate sacrifice, there have been the many unnumbered Americans who have quietly gone about making their sacrifices in innumerable ways, many even giving their lives, without acknowledgement.

Well, the question I have asked myself, even as a teenage boy in a foxhole in the Pacific theater of war, is "What makes men willing to pledge their lives to this country?" I believe President Lincoln knew. So did the thousands of others who have joined him in death for the cause of truth and freedom. Lincoln said:

"This love of liberty which God has planted in us constitutes the bulwark of our liberty and independence. It is not our form in battlements, or bristling sea coasts, or only in our Navy. Our defense is in the spirit which prizes liberty as the heritage of all men in all lands everywhere. Destroy this spirit, and we have planted the seeds of despotism at our own doors."

There's the answer! It is the love of liberty which motivates our allegiance to America. God planted it in all of us. If we nurture it, it never dies. But it can die if we're not careful.

Where do we start? What do we do to make sure the light and spirit of liberty within each of us does remain? What will make us "pledge our allegiance" unwaveringly to this nation? Laying down our lives may not be necessary. In fact, I pray that we may never be required to do so. But in one way or another we can do something—many things—to keep that spirit alive.

I am reminded of a young boy in a supermarket. While waiting at the checkout counter, he was carefully examining several pieces of candy. The clerk, somewhat impatient with him for holding up the line of customers, said rather gruffly, "Come on, sonny, hurry up; make up your mind!" The boy looked up at the clerk and said, "Please don't rush me. I have only four cents to spend."

Now, like the young lad, you and I may have only limited resources and abilities, but we can spend them wisely! We can carefully examine our lives and see what needs to be spent to keep the spirit of liberty alive in our hearts. Here are some simple choices. We can:

1. Vote.
2. Attend our neighborhood mass meetings.
3. Keep track of our political representatives and write to them when appropriate.

4. Display the flag on special occasions (or even daily).
5. Pray for our elected officials, especially the president of our country.
6. Teach our children to love this great nation.
7. Pay an honest income tax (now there's a challenge for some)!
8. Obey the laws of the land.
9. Run for office.
10. Talk positively about the freedoms we enjoy.

The list goes on. You and I can do at least some of these things. Wouldn't it be wonderful if we could do them all?

I suppose it all boils down to Shakespeare's words in his epic *Hamlet:*

> This above all—to thine own self be true;
> And it must follow, as the night the day,
> Thou canst not then be false to any man.
> (Act 1, scene 3, lines 78–80.)

God has truly implanted in each one of us the spirit of liberty. If we're true to that spirit, we'll be all right. In fact, we'll be great! Our allegiance may be demonstrated in small ways, or we may be called upon to give our lives. But either way, I bear witness that God will know of our sacrifice, and He will reward us personally and as a country, both now and forever.

May I, with you, take this opportunity once again to pledge my great love, support, and loyalty for and to the United States of America; and may we, together, hold fast and firm to this promise, for our own sakes and for the sake of this nation.

" *Liberty is power. . . ; the nation blessed with the largest portion of liberty will be the most powerful nation upon the earth.* "

JOHN QUINCY ADAMS

" *Those who expect to reap the blessings of freedom must, like men, undergo the fatigues of supporting it.* "

THOMAS PAINE

" *We have a right to be proud of our Pilgrim and Puritan fathers. . . . They were ready to do and to suffer anything for their faith, and a faith which breeds heroes is better than an unbelief which leaves nothing worth being a hero for.* "

OLIVER WENDELL HOLMES

" *As long as our government is administered for the good of the people, and is regulated by their will; as long as it secures to us the rights of persons and of property, liberty of conscience and of the press, it will be worth defending.* "

ANDREW JACKSON

" *The last hopes of mankind rest with us; and if it should be proclaimed that our example had become an argument against the experiment, the knell of popular liberty would be sounded throughout the earth.* "

DANIEL WEBSTER

CHAPTER 3

ONE OF OUR
GREATEST BLESSINGS

Recently I came upon a very short document which started me thinking; I would invite you to reflect on its few lines. As you read them, ask yourself if you would be willing to accept the terms contained therein. It is called the "Oath of American Citizenship." I am sure similar oaths exist in most countries of the world. Would you and I and our children be willing to abide by its precepts? Here is the oath:

"I hereby declare, on oath, that I absolutely and entirely renounce and abjure all allegiance and fidelity to any foreign prince, potentate, state, or citizen; that I will support and defend the Constitution and laws of the United States of America against all enemies, foreign and domestic; that I will bear true faith and allegiance to the same; and that I take this obligation freely without any mental reservation or purpose of evasion: so help me God." (54 U.S. St. L. 1157.)

Those are great words! Imagine what you would do if you were not a citizen of this country and were asked to raise your right hand and repeat that oath. Might I suggest that doing just that as a family might not be a bad idea? It would be a great thing to have that oath posted somewhere in our homes where we could occasionally look at it.

Did you notice that in the Oath of American Citizenship there is no allegiance to individuals but only to the Constitution? I find that reassuring. One of the great defenders of our American heritage, President J. Reuben Clark, Jr., stated: "God provided that in this land of liberty, our political allegiance shall run not to individuals, that is, to government officials, no matter how great or how small they may be. Under His plan our allegiance and the only allegiance we owe as citizens or denizens of the United States, runs to our inspired Constitution which God Himself set up. So runs the oath of office of those who participate in government. A certain loyalty we do owe to the office which a man holds, but even here we owe, just by reason of our citizenship, no loyalty to the man himself. In other countries it is to the individual that allegiance runs. This principle of allegiance to the Constitution is basic to our freedom. It is one of the great principles that distinguishes this 'land of liberty' from other countries." (*Messages of the First Presidency*, comp. James R. Clark [Salt Lake City: Bookcraft, 1975], 6:107.)

I suppose that President Clark would not have made such statements if he had not been convinced that this nation was founded by a kind and wise Heavenly Father. I share that same conviction. My own parents had a great love for and appreciation of America. They spent much time as my brothers and I were growing up citing experiences of our country's history, of the great contributions made to its freedom by our Founding Fathers, and of the divine nature of the Constitution. On one occasion my father shared with us an account which Thomas Jefferson once gave concerning the Declaration of Independence:

"On that day of our nation's birth in the little hall in Philadelphia, debate had raged for hours. The men gathered there were honorable men hard-pressed by a king who had flouted the very laws they were willing to obey. Even so, to sign a declaration of independence was such an irretrievable act that the walls resounded with the words *treason, the gallows, the headsman's axe,* and the issue remained in doubt.

"Then a man rose and spoke. Jefferson described him as not a young man, but one who had to summon all his energy for an impassioned plea. He cited the grievances that had brought them to this moment, and finally, his voice failing, he said, 'They may turn every tree into a gallows, every home into a grave, and yet the words of that parchment can never die. To the mechanic in the workshop, they will speak hope; to the slave in the mines, freedom. Sign that parchment. Sign if the next moment the noose is around your neck, for that parchment will be the textbook of freedom, the Bible of the rights of man forever.'

"He fell back exhausted. The fifty-six delegates, swept up by his eloquence, rushed forward and signed a document destined to be as immortal as a work of man can be. When they turned to thank him for his timely oratory, he was not to be found, nor could any be found who knew who he was or how he had come in or gone out through the locked and guarded doors."

Now, some may scoff at such a story, but I believe it to be true, nevertheless. The Lord did that and more to secure this land of freedom. His hand has been upon this country from the beginning.

As a young seminary teacher I came upon a bit of wisdom from Elder Orson Hyde which validated what I had always believed about the founding of our country and which has been verified by the reality of my firsthand combat against one of America's foes. Elder Hyde's comment is fascinating:

"In those early and perilous times, our men were few, and our resources limited. Poverty was among the most potent enemies we had to encounter; yet our arms were successful; and it may not be amiss to ask here, by whose power victory so often perched on our banner? It was by the agency of that same angel of God that appeared unto Joseph Smith, and revealed to him the history of the early inhabitants of this country. . . . This same angel presides over the destinies of America, and feels a lively interest in all our doings. He was in the camp of Washington; and, by an invisible hand, led on our fathers to conquest and victory. . . .

"This same angel was with Columbus, and gave him deep impressions, by dreams and by visions, respecting this New World. Trammelled by poverty and by an unpopular cause, yet his persevering and unyielding heart would not allow an obstacle in his way too great for him to overcome; and the angel of God helped him—was with him on the stormy deep, calmed the troubled elements, and guided his frail vessel to the desired haven. Under the guardianship of this same angel, or Prince of America, have the United States grown, increased, and flourished, like the sturdy oak by the rivers of water." (*Journal of Discourses,* 6:362.)

I submit, however, that inspiration alone did not found this country. The individual courage of the people, over and over again, moved us along. Shortly after the founding of this nation, a little-known incident brought into focus what it would take if this country were to continue to exist:

"A young Hungarian named Koscia had fled after the abortive uprising against the emperor of Austria-Hungary, taking out his first citizenship papers in this country. He became an importer. He was in a Mediterranean port on business when he was recognized and taken aboard an Austrian flagship in the harbor for return to the empire to be tried as a traitor. His frantic manservant recognized a flag he had heard his master describe as now his flag—the Stars and Stripes. It was carried by a small American war sloop. He told the story of his master's fate to the captain of this small vessel.

"Captain Ingram went ashore and repeated the story to the American consul. Then, without waiting for the slow, diplomatic wheels to turn, he went aboard the Austrian flagship and demanded to see the American citizen they held. The Austrian admiral must have been somewhat amused when the prisoner was brought on deck in chains and the upstart American captain said he could hear the prisoner better without those chains. The chains were removed.

"Then Captain Ingram asked Koscia one question: 'Do you ask the protection of the American flag?' And the answer was yes. He said, 'You shall have it.'

"Going ashore once again, he told the consul of his action. By this time it had been learned that Koscia had only taken out his first application for citizenship. The consul's reaction was that we should wash our hands of the affair. Captain Ingram disagreed.

"As the day went on, two more Austrian warships sailed into the harbor and it began to look as if all three ships were preparing to depart. Captain Ingram sent a messenger to the Austrian admiral. He said, 'Any effort to leave this port with our citizen will be resisted with appropriate force. I will expect a satisfactory answer by four o'clock this afternoon.'

"As the hour approached, the little war sloop stood ringed by the three giant warships. Captain Ingram ordered the guns rolled to the open ports. Then he ordered the tapers lighted with which the cannons were to be fired. At that moment, a lookout called down from the mast and said, 'They're lowering a boat.' Koscia was delivered to Captain Ingram, who then went below and wrote his letter of resignation to the United States Navy.

"He said if he had embarrassed his country, this was all he could do, but the action he had taken, he believed, was in keeping with his oath as an officer. His resignation was turned down by the United States Senate with these words, 'This battle that was never fought may turn out to be the most important battle in our nation's history.' "

Inspiration and courage together are an unbeatable team—a team that has worked for athletes, for artists, for statesmen, and for our great nation.

Now, there is some danger in discussing for too long such an elevated subject without losing focus. Occasionally we need to put things into perspective. Just for a moment, let's get down to the basics. What is this free nation all about? Why is it worth defending? Why should we subscribe to an oath of citizenship that requires so much effort? Let me share a short excerpt from the life of a Russian immigrant. (The occasion was a trip by train from San Francisco to New York.) From her perspective the story went something like this:

"One day, I left San Francisco by train for New York. The next morning I had my first American breakfast. I was in the diner car, sitting at the same table with very successful-looking businessmen. You know, the kind of businessmen who, when they pick up a menu, never look to the right. They just read to the left. When I pick up a menu, I study carefully the right and then I switch to the left. When I needed sugar for my coffee, I didn't know that in restaurants and diners they packed each piece of sugar separately. I looked around. I didn't want to ask the businessmen. Well, it was a nice, big silver gadget. I picked it up and shook its contents in my coffee. The businessmen asked me, 'I beg your pardon. Why do you put salt in your coffee?' I was ashamed of my mistake, but I looked straight in his eyes and said, 'You know, a very famous doctor in Russia discovered if you drink one cup of coffee with salt in the morning, you stay young and slim as long as you live!' I finished my coffee and departed. It was horrible."

We can now add salt-free coffee to our list of defendable items.

Now, I know that this story is simple, but it makes a point. If you and I are willingly going to do what we talked about in the Oath of American Citizenship, we must have a cause. I suggest that we have one. Inspiration and courage in the defense of such a small thing as salt-free coffee is one of the things it's all about.

Now, let's talk about another side of the precious freedom we enjoy—the freedom to be different, to think and feel differently about many things. This basic right, if carried to the extreme, can sometimes lead to trouble in the land. In one of the greatest musicals of our time, *The Music Man,* the central character sings these words from a lively number in the show: "We got trouble, right here in River City." Allow me to repeat those words one more time: "We got trouble, right here in River City." May I suggest that "we got trouble" right here in our cities—your city, my city, and all cities. We've also got trouble in Idaho, Montana, California, North Dakota, Minnesota, Alabama, New Jersey, and Washington, D.C. Our major problem isn't with Libya, Africa, Russia, or China. It's not with India or Pakistan, Lebanon or Nicaragua. It's with the thinking of some of our own people.

Cicero never heard *The Music Man,* but he knew trouble when he saw it. He said, "A nation can survive its fools and even its ambitions, but it cannot survive treason from within."

Abraham Lincoln put it a little differently but still hit the mark: "At what point, then, is the approach to danger to be expected? If it even reaches us it must spring up among us. It cannot come from abroad. If destruction be our lot, we must ourselves be its author and finisher; as a nation of freemen, we must live through all time or die by suicide." (Springfield, Illinois, January 27, 1827.) Not bad advice from two men who never sang in a Broadway musical!

May I affirm that the danger to our nation is real. Not too long ago a convention was held at one of this nation's largest universities. Representatives came from all over the United States. One of the most sobering moments occurred when two young women came down the aisle with two flags. One was the red flag of communism; the other was the black flag of anarchy. Eight hundred delegates stood and cheered.

My purpose here is not to cite case after case of potential or real treason—you can read about those incidents in the newspapers and see them in your own communities. My aim is to bear witness of the divine origin of this country, to raise a question, propose a solution, and have us all think seriously about it.

The question is: What are we going to do about all of the internal strife in our land?

David O. McKay emphasized the importance of that question with these words: "Next to being one in worshipping God, there is nothing in this world upon which this church should be more united than in upholding and defending the Constitution of the United States!" (TL, 10:41.) Each one of us can make a difference. George Bernard Shaw put it clearly in two short sentences: "Liberty means responsibility. That is why most men dread it." I believe with all my heart that most of us aren't afraid of the responsibility of freedom. I believe we welcome it.

I know two things we can do during the coming year that will help stem the decay of our American heritage and way of life.

My first suggestion comes from President Lincoln. On March 30, 1863, he proclaimed a "National Fast Day." Included in his remarks was this inspired counsel: "We have been preserved these many years in peace and prosperity. We have grown in numbers, wealth, and power as no other nation has ever grown. But we have forgotten God. We have forgotten the gracious hand which preserved us in peace, and multiplied and enriched and strengthened us; and we have vainly imagined, in the deceitfulness of our hearts, that all these blessings were produced by some superior wisdom and virtue of our own. Intoxicated with unbroken success, we have become too self-sufficient to feel the necessity of redeeming and preserving grace, too proud to pray to the God that made us!

"It behooves us then to humble ourselves before the offended power, to confess our national sins, and to pray for clemency and forgiveness." (*The Collected Words of Abraham Lincoln,* vol. 6, pp. 155–56.)

This wise counsel, then, is the first thing I believe we should follow. Before we attempt to improve, why don't we acknowledge our need to do so? I sincerely believe that if each person, each couple, each family would continually and prayerfully acknowledge our need for His help, not only as individuals and families but as a nation, He would give it to us. I am a firm believer in repentance. I've had to do my share. I feel strongly that if we would repent in humility, our neighborhoods and communities would become better. And we would find ourselves more aware of the principles of freedom around us and would be much more likely to defend them. Now, does that sound too difficult?

My second suggestion is equally simple. It comes from a man named Dean Alfange. I take delight in sharing it: "I do not choose to be a common man. It is my right to be uncommon—if I can. I seek opportunity [to develop whatever talents God gave me]—not security. I do not wish to be a kept citizen, humbled and dulled by having the state look after me. I want to take the calculated risk; to dream and to build, to fail and to succeed. I refuse to barter incentive for a dole. I prefer the challenges of life to the guaranteed existence; the thrill of fulfillment to the stale calm of Utopia. I will not trade freedom for beneficence nor my dignity for a handout. I will never cower before any earthly master nor bend to any threat. It is my heritage to stand erect, proud and unafraid; to think and act for myself, enjoy the benefit of my creations, and to face the world boldly and say—'This, with God's help, I have done.' All this is what it means to be an American." (From "Dean Alfange," *Who's Who in America,* vol. 1, 44th ed. [Wilmette, Illinois: Macmillan, 1986–87], p. 37.)

Well, that's my second suggestion—that we become uncommon in our pursuit of a seemingly common opportunity; that we can become uncommonly good in the pursuit of our freedom and its opportunities; that we not settle for less than we are capable. When we are willing to dream and plan, succeed and fail, we are on our way. Such a course will preserve the liberty and responsibility that Shaw mentioned.

If you and I would do those two simple things during this coming year, we could have a profound effect on the entire country. Why don't we give it a try?

I conclude this chapter with a little verse by Edgar A. Guest. It has been a favorite of many:

> To serve my country day by day
> At any humble post I may;
> To honor and respect her Flag,
> To live the traits of which I brag;
> To be American in deed
> As well as in my printed creed.
>
> To stand for truth and honest toil,
> To till my little patch of soil
> And keep in mind the debt I owe
> To them who died, that I might know
> My country, prosperous and free,
> And passed this heritage to me.
>
> I must always in trouble's hour
> Be guided by the men in power;
> For God and country I must live,
> My best for God and country give;
> No act of mine that men may scan
> Must shame the name American.
>
> To do my best and play my part,
> American in mind and heart;
> To serve the flag and bravely stand
> To guard the glory of my land;
> To be American in deed;
> God grant me strength to keep this creed.
> ("A Patriotic Creed," *Over Here* [Chicago:
> the Reilly and Lee Co., 1918], p. 40.)

Let us think seriously about our citizenship and the responsibility it carries. May we also find the courage to take positive action in defending that commitment and heritage. May we often repeat and live the Oath of American Citizenship, which I believe to be one of our greatest blessings.

❝ The American people have never taken fear for a counsellor. They have never taken doubt for a guide. They have obeyed the impulses of their blood. They have hearkened to the voice of our God. . . . Let American statesmanship listen to the heartbeats of the American people in the present hour and there will be no confusion, no hesitation, no craven doubt. The courage of Lexington and Bunker Hill is with us yet. The unconquerable heart of the pioneer still beats within American breasts. The American people are the propagandists and not the misers of liberty. The American people are not perishing; they are just beginning their real career. ❞

ALBERT J. BEVERIDGE

❝ Let the words go forth from this time and place, to friend and foe alike, that the torch has been passed to a new generation of Americans—born in this century, tempered by war, disciplined by a hard and bitter peace, proud of our ancient heritage—and unwilling to witness or permit the slow undoing of those human rights to which this nation is committed today at home and around the world.
Let every nation know, whether it wishes us well or ill, that we shall pay any price, bear any burden, meet any hardship, support any friend, oppose any foe to assure the survival and the success of liberty.
This much we pledge—and more. ❞

JOHN F. KENNEDY

CHAPTER 4

A WORD
OF GRATITUDE

In homes throughout the land, members of many families, whether belonging to any organized religious group or not, often share a spiritual, special experience. These family members frequently bow their heads to give thanks, not only for their food and the bounties of life, but also for countless other blessings enjoyed. When participated in with hearts full of humble and sincere feelings, these experiences in prayerful thanksgiving can be rich and rewarding. However, it is also possible that, though the original intent might be sincere, such attempts at gratitude can become ritualistic and routine.

Some of us may become so dulled by privilege, so taken by pleasure, so overcome by self-preoccupation that a grateful heart is just out of reach. Or some may be just too worried to be grateful, noting that a simple meal costs more this year than last and that one's job seems less secure. But if counting your blessings seems strained this year for any reason, take note of this true story.

The newspaper columnist Jack Anderson learned, before it became common knowledge, that the people of Cambodia were being systematically dispossessed, driven from their homes, or even slaughtered. He wrote about this human desecration in his columns, but nobody seemed to listen or believe. It was too horrible to comprehend, too much to fathom.

Meanwhile, a young man named Pol and his wife and two children had had their lives disrupted and torn apart. They were taken from their homes and put in a concentration camp. Since the food allotment was too small to sustain them all, Pol gave his ration to his children and lived on rats and snakes. This was still not enough, and he watched his children slowly dying before his eyes. Their skin became tight over their bones, their rib cages showed, and their thin necks and sunken eyes made them look like starving birds.

Pol wrote several letters to his sister in America, telling her of their awful situation. Trying to help, she wrote back, but her letters never got to him. Finally, she received a letter from him saying that he had given up hope and thought it best that he kill his wife and children and commit suicide. (Anything was better than starving to death or being slaughtered.)

The sister, frantic at receiving such news, managed to contact Jack Anderson, since he had been writing about the subject. Mr. Anderson decided that even if he couldn't save millions of Cambodians with his articles, he could save one family. He spent three days making phone calls and pulling strings. Within two weeks a miracle had happened. Pol and his little family were on a plane to the United States.

As Pol and his sister were reunited in Las Vegas, the air was heavy with emotion, so much so that the family drove speechless most of the way to their new home in southern Utah. This home was an arid wasteland of desert and sagebrush, a place where most Americans would decline to live. For Pol, however, this was heaven on earth. When they arrived at their destination and the door to the van was opened, Pol finally spoke. He didn't know any English, so his was not an eloquent speech. But he did know one word. As he exited the van he looked around him with fervent emotion and raised his arms with fists clenched. Like a football player who has just made the winning touchdown at the Superbowl, Pol leaped into the air and cried out his one word of triumph—*"America!"*

America! We can see that one word of gratitude in the smile of Winn, a beautiful Indo-Chinese refugee who has been in this country only six months. She has mothered eleven children, held them close, stroked their cheeks with a tender touch. And she has lost all of them but three. At least she thinks she has three left. Her two sons, ages thirteen and fourteen, were taken by the invading armies in Laos two years ago and she hasn't seen them since. Her husband was taken, too, to work along the lines. She assumes he is dead, for the normal course has been to take the men, feed them little, and work them to death. Winn's daughter is with her still, but at twenty-one she has been so ravaged by war and death and hunger that she has withdrawn into herself, a shadow of the vibrant girl she might have been.

America! Bounlom walks with confidence and an eye to the future. To get here he first had to swim the Mekong River under fear for his life. Every morning for a time, the Mekong River had in it the bodies of those who had tried to escape during the night and were not as lucky as he. Bounlom then spent four years in a refugee camp waiting for his chance to come to this country. He finally left Laos at seventeen and is still haunted with worry about his aged parents who were left behind. He has sent to a brother in France every penny of the money he earned during his first three months here, hoping the brother, too, can come to America.

Stories like these are sobering, but they do help us to confront the essential facts of life. If we have trouble in this challenging world thinking of one word of gratitude, let it be *America*. It is more than just a country, it's a concept. It is based on the idea that when people are given the freedom to be themselves, to be unpretentious or grand, enterprising or less ambitious, wonderful things can happen. We have a government of the people, by the people, and for the people, basically because we trust the people. The people have all the power except that which they themselves decide to grant to the government.

We have the opportunity to make good laws, and, if they aren't good laws, to correct them. We believe that integrity does more to rule a society than police forces. We believe that we all have within ourselves a spark that can propel us as far as our energy and dreams will allow.

Here in America, when we go to sleep at night, we are not worried that an army will come and snatch away a family member. Most of us do not seriously wonder if we will go hungry tomorrow. If we don't like something, we can speak up, lobby, criticize. And our leaders know that they are subject to the close scrutiny of the public who elected them. We believe in freedom, not overregulation; in consensus, not power plays. Surprisingly enough, these idealistic notions have helped us achieve a stable government that has faced crisis and confrontation and has always stood firm.

The pilgrims who celebrated that first Thanksgiving were refugees from tyranny, just as are the refugees I have described. The pilgrims lost well over one-third of their number before that Thanksgiving day, but they still found something to be grateful about. America—enough to eat, a place to be yourself; Indian or pilgrim, Indo-Chinese or Polish—the legacy of freedom and security continues.

So with yesterday's pilgrims and today's refugees, let's be humbly and sincerely grateful for America. And if we are, let's get involved; let our voices be heard so that we can keep it the kind of America for which we will always be grateful.

> Teach me, Father, when I pray,
> Not to ask for more,
> But rather let me give my thanks
> For what is at my door.
>
> (Anonymous)

I am indeed thankful for America and for the many blessings it offers.

*"Equal rights for all. . . .
Special privileges for none."*

THOMAS JEFFERSON

*"They have a right to censure,
that have a heart to help."*

WILLIAM PENN

*"Rome endured as long as there were Romans.
America will endure as long as we remain American in
spirit and thought."*

WILLIAM GEORGE JORDAN

*"Americanism consists in utterly believing in the
principles of America."*

WOODROW WILSON

"One country, one constitution, one destiny . . ."

DANIEL WEBSTER

CHAPTER 5

OUR GREATEST
WEAPON

There is something very special about America. We sometimes hear it referred to as the land of liberty. It is also often called the land of freedom. It can be called many things, I suppose. But I am hearing more and more patriotic speeches refer to freedom, liberty, and America without mentioning the most important element of all. It's almost as if some are ashamed of certain key words. There are those who would have us eliminate these words altogether. But if we do, our nation is headed for deep trouble. Those missing words are *goodness* and *righteousness.* Alexis de Tocqueville, the famous French historian, wrote in his book *Democracy in America:*

"I sought for the greatness and genius of America in her commodious harbors and her ample rivers, and it was not there; in her fertile fields and boundless prairies, and it was not there; in her rich mines and her vast world of commerce, and it was not there. Not until I went to the churches of America and heard her pulpits aflame with righteousness did I understand the secret of her genius and power. America is great because she is good, and if America ever ceases to be good, America will cease to be great."

I firmly believe there is a reason that America is good. There are reasons that this nation came into being.

The founding of this nation and the goodness of her people are inseparably connected. George Washington, first president of our nation, in his inaugural address to Congress, stressed God's part in the birth of this republic:

"No people can be bound to acknowledge and adore the invisible hand which conducts the affairs of men more than the people of the United States. Every step by which they have advanced to the character of an independent nation seems to have been distinguished by some token of providential agency—we ought to be no less persuaded that the propitious smiles of heaven cannot be expected on a nation that disregards the eternal rules of order and right, which heaven itself has ordained."

Later, Abraham Lincoln added:

"It is the duty of nations, as well as of men, to owe their dependence upon the overruling power of God and to recognize the sublime truth announced in the holy scriptures and proven by all history, that those nations only are blessed whose God is the Lord."

It is an interesting study to look at the foundations of this land and hear in the voices of those great patriots the recognition that they believed God's hand was in the affairs that transpired.

Remember Columbus? In the very discovery of this Land, God's influence was recognized. In writing to the Spanish leaders Columbus said: "Our Lord unlocked my mind, sent me upon the sea, and gave me fire for the deed. Those who heard of my enterprise called it foolish, mocked me, and laughed. But who can doubt but that the Holy Ghost inspired me?" (Jacob Wassermann, *Columbus: Don Quixote of the Seas* [Boston: Little, Brown and Co., 1930], p. 20.)

Time passed. Then, as America struggled to become free, some of the greatest men ever to walk the earth raised their voices in defense of God and country. Patrick Henry was not the least of these. Just before the signing of the Declaration of Independence he talked of God. Note his comments:

"Yes, were my soul trembling on the wing of eternity, were this hand freezing to death, were my voice choking with the last struggle, I would still, with the last gasp of that voice, implore you to remember the truth. God has given America to be free.

Others who spoke in defense of America were John Adams, Alexander Hamilton, John Hancock, and Benjamin Harrison. As president of the United States, Thomas Jefferson added his voice in his belief of God and this country: "I have sworn upon the altar of God eternal hostility against every form of tyranny over the mind of man."

As the Constitution of the United States came into being, Benjamin Franklin gave his support to the deliberations of the representatives of the colonies. Listen to these great words:

"I have lived a long time, and the longer I live, the more convincing proofs I see of this truth: that God governs in the affairs of men. And if a sparrow cannot fall to the ground without his notice, is it probable that an empire can rise without his aid?

"We have been assured, sir, in the sacred writings, that 'except the Lord build the house, they labour in vain that build it . . .' (Psalm 127:1). I firmly believe this; and I also believe that without his concurring aid we shall succeed in this political building no better than the builders of Babel. We shall be divided by our little partial local interest, our products will be confounded, and we ourselves shall become a reproach and byword down to future ages. And, what is worse, mankind may hereafter from this unfortunate instance despair of establishing governments by human wisdom and leave it to chance, war, and conquest.

"I therefore beg leave to move that henceforth prayers imploring the assistance of heaven and its blessings on our deliberations be held in this assembly every morning before we proceed to business, and that one or more of the clergy of this city be requested to officiate in that service."

John Quincy Adams declared: "Posterity—you will never know how much it has cost my generation to preserve your freedom. I hope you will make good use of it."

Thomas Paine said, "What we obtain too cheaply, we esteem too lightly; it is dearness only that gives everything its value. Heaven knows how to put a price upon its goods; and it would be strange indeed if so celestial an article as freedom should not be highly rated."

Daniel Webster reminded us:

"Lastly, our ancestors established their system of government on morality and religious sentiment. Moral habits, they believed, cannot safely be trusted on any other foundation than religious principle, nor any government be secure which is not supported by moral habits.

"We often forget that, in declaring independence from an earthly power, our forefathers made a forthright declaration of dependence upon Almighty God. The closing words of this document solemnly declare: 'With a firm reliance on the protection of divine providence, we mutually pledge to each other our lives, our fortunes, and our sacred honor.'

"The fifty-six courageous men who signed that document not only understood that pledge but many, through tremendous hardship, war, and death at the hands of the British, paid the price. They considered liberty much more important than the security they enjoyed. They fulfilled their pledge. They paid the price. And freedom was won. Someone has said, 'To be born free is a privilege. To die free is an awesome responsibility.' "

How could the Constitutional Convention fail with such men? It was the Lord Himself who said: "Therefore, it is not right that any man should be in bondage one to another. And for this purpose have I established the Constitution of this land, by the hands of wise men whom I raised up unto this very purpose." (D&C 101:79–80.)

From one generation to another, great patriots have spoken of God and America. You cannot separate them. Some will try, but it cannot be done. Voices from the past and the present attest to the fact.

And so, what do we do in our day to see to it that a belief in God is paramount to an understanding of America? President Harold B. Lee joined Columbus, Washington, Lincoln, and others when he said:

"Speaking of liberty . . . man possesses human dignity because he is made in the image and likeness of God; it is this image that makes man different, that makes man a son of God. Without this image, man has no free will and, frequently, neither liberty nor the capacity for liberty. . . . In this struggle for freedom, at home or abroad, our greatest weapon, both a sword and a shield, will be our love of and faith in God." (Harold B. Lee, BYU Devotional.)

Once more a great leader has urged us to place God and America in the same sentence.

You and I can do much to see that God and America go together. Our greatest weapon of liberty is "a love of and faith in God." We must put righteousness where it belongs. The sword of goodness is our greatest weapon.

Edward Sill wrote this verse describing a dream he had of a furious battle in which a prince's banner

Wavered, then staggered backward, hemmed
    by foes.
A craven hung along the battle's edge,
And thought, "Had I a sword of keener steel—
That blue blade that the King's son bears—but this
Blunt thing—!" He snapped and flung it from his
    hand,
And lowering crept away and left the field.

Then came the King's son, wounded, sore bestead,
And weaponless, and saw the broken sword,
Hilt-buried in the dry and trodden sand,
And ran and snatched it; and with a battle-shout
Lifted afresh he hewed his enemy down,
And saved a great cause that heroic day.
("Opportunity," *Library of World's Great Literature,* vol. 23, ed. Chas. Dudley Warner [New York: J.A. Hill & Co., 1896], p. 13441.)

Americans need to pick up again the sword of righteousness and hold it high for all the world to see. You and I can lift that sword of truth and proclaim with pride to all who will listen. Our voices can be raised with Jefferson and Lincoln and modern patriots. America will endure as long as Americans believe in and love God. If we love him, we will be righteous. As long as we are, then that great lady's symbol in New York's harbor will really mean something:

Give me your tired, your poor,
Your huddled masses yearning to breathe free,
The wretched refuse of your teeming shore,
Send these, the homeless, tempest-tossed to me,
I lift my lamp beside the golden door.
                                        (Emma Lazarus)

Do you recall the question posed by the French historian Guizot to James Russell Lowell? "How long will the American republic endure?" asked Guizot. Lowell's answer: "As long as the ideas of the men who founded it continue dominant."

Do you understand his answer? "As long as the ideas of the men who founded it continue dominant."

You and I know that central to everything concerning America, her past, and her future, is the belief that God founded this nation and that goodness is paramount. As long as Americans believe and practice that belief, we will be preserved.

Finally, I do not pretend to be matched with the greats, but I too am a patriot! I know and understand the price of freedom. I have stood in battle to defend America. If need be I would do it again. But we can all take up the sword of truth and righteousness and proclaim it in our homes, schools, and churches. We can declare it in deed and by example. May we in our own humble and quiet way proclaim to the world how the divine hand of providence is still molding America.

" There is nothing wrong with America that the faith, love of freedom, intelligence, and energy of her citizens cannot cure. "

DWIGHT D. EISENHOWER

" Men and times change—but principles—never! "

GROVER CLEVELAND

" Of all the work that is done or that can be done for our country, the greatest is that of educating the body, the mind, and above all the character, giving spiritual and moral training to those who in a few years are themselves to decide the destinies of the nation. "

THEODORE ROOSEVELT

" Whether you be men or women, you will never do anything in the world without courage. It is the greatest quality of the mind next to honor. "

JAMES ALLEN

" A man of courage is also full of faith. "

CICERO

" I honor any man who in the conscious discharge of his duty dares to stand alone. "

CHARLES SUMNER

CHAPTER 6

THE QUALITY OF COURAGE

When John F. Kennedy was president, he gathered together for dinner one evening a brain trust of the best and the brightest in the country to examine the nation and its problems. At one point in the evening, he looked at the crowd assembled and observed with a smile that the White House hadn't seen such a mingling of brilliance and talent since Thomas Jefferson dined there alone.

We often think back with a kind of nostalgia to those legendary men and women who have made this nation great, and to many it seems that no one today quite equals the giants of the past. We look around desperately to see someone with the nobility of an Abraham Lincoln, the patriotism of a Patrick Henry, the common sense of a Thomas Paine, the courage of a

George Washington as he led his men through the terrible winter at Valley Forge. Too many of us believe that the American people have become a spineless group, unable any more to produce individuals of that stature. But I don't believe it! I think they exist all around us, maybe sometimes unseen, but nonetheless present.

For anyone who has ever wondered if America has lost its will and courage, consider for a moment the members of the Congressional Medal of Honor Society. Do you know about them? Since the Civil War, Congress has awarded 3308 men the Congressional Medal of Honor for exceptional bravery in battle. There are 275 medal holders still living among us—10 from World War I, 144 from World War II, 38 from the Korean War, and 83 from the war in Vietnam. The requirements for receiving the medal read like this: "The deed of the person must be proved by incontestable evidence of at least two eyewitnesses; it must be so outstanding that it clearly distinguishes his gallantry from lesser forms of bravery; it must involve the risk of his life, and it must be the type of deed which, if he had not done it, would not subject him to any justified criticism."

It is impossible to read each individual citation without being overcome with the valor of these soldiers. One had "saved the lives of his men at the sacrifice of his life by throwing himself directly on a mine as it exploded." Others had stood up and fired at the enemy in the face of almost certain death. These are typical descriptions, not unusual ones. In every instance personal survival had taken a back seat to saving the lives of others.

Who are these heroes and where are they now? Hank Whittemore, a novelist, decided to attend their biennial reunion and see for himself what kind of men had bravery enough in the clinch to deserve such a citation. Who are these men who would throw themselves upon grenades to save a fellow and then disappear among us disguised as our next-door neighbor?

As Whittemore attended the reunion, one thing became immediately obvious. There were no corps of press, no flashing lights, no surge of television reporters eager for just one word from these exceptional men. No, the Congressional Medal of Honor Reunion went largely unnoticed. But there was something else as tangible as a camera among them; it was a kind of electricity, a secret that every one of these men carried and could share, in many ways, only with each other, for they had been there where so many of us will never tread. They had faced the ultimate test of themselves and had pulled from some silent chamber of their soul a will to fight against whatever the odds for a higher cause. Whittemore decided it was a secret worth discovering, and he followed the medal holders through their banquet and their speeches trying to learn just what their secret was. What is courage anyway?

Some things became evident immediately. The men—some of whom were missing limbs and others who carried scars from burns—all admitted that they had been afraid. Their special deeds were performed despite a terrible awareness of the danger involved and a knowledge of what was at stake. But they had handled their fear, noted the gravity of the situation, and risen to it.

Part of the reason they had risen to it was that they got angry. One man, standing alone, had gotten mad at the course of events and had said, in effect, "I won't let this happen! This is not the way things are supposed to be." And by his action he made all the difference.

But there was something more, even beyond the fear, beyond the anger. Whittemore said it this way: "Underneath the fear and the anger, there had been a dedication to others. This sort of courage—perhaps courage itself—is not selfish. It regards comrades' lives as more valuable than one's own. It means being willing to crawl back into a flaming helicopter to save the pilot; diving down to a submarine to rescue those who are trapped; instead of fleeing for safety, racing out to treat the wounded and helpless and dragging them away from the bullets."

Whittemore continued, "Courage, I found, is not the result of a contest. You don't 'win' the Medal of Honor. You have a certain amount of training and experience, but then comes an event that calls for spontaneous action. You either respond in a certain way or you don't. You cannot predict, ever, what you will do. Not a single medal holder was aware, beforehand, that he really had the 'guts' to be a hero."

One can't pick out a hero just by looking at him. A hero bears no distinguishing marks, does not walk with a certain bravado. He looks just like the rest of us. But hidden in his soul, as secret as the wound that many medal holders carry, there is something special, something that may not show itself without a test. But in the clinch, in that moment from whence there is no turning back, the hero does not shrink away to save himself: he flings himself into the fight; he knows what courage is.

Now, we are living in a time that calls for courage. It is a time that tests our very mettle, that shows us up for what we really are. Do we live for more than self-serving ends? Is there something fundamental in us that responds to a higher value than self-gratification? The future of our country depends upon that answer. It depends upon our courage in many small ways, everyday courage absent the battle.

A country whose people have the will to live for something more than selfishness is ultimately a strong nation. A country whose people will be directed by unchanging moral values instead of the shiftlessness of the moment will survive any crisis. This is America, a nation of heroes who have always fought and lived for the highest values mankind has held. It has been a beacon for the whole world, and it will continue to be if we believe in ourselves, if we truly understand, like the Medal of Honor winners, that in any battle one soul can make a difference.

This is not a time for hopelessness. It is a time for heroism. The best history of this country is still in the making. It is not just a misty memory of years gone by. The best people are still emerging. It has long been my prayer that we will have the courage to be as patriotic in our own way as the Congressional Medal of Honor winners and insightful enough to understand why we ought to be. There's no country quite like America!

PART II

BROADENING
HORIZONS

PURSUIT OF LIBERTY

Freedom Is . . .

66 *Freedom is a man at the lathe, or at the desk, doing the job he likes to do, and speaking up for himself. It is a man in the pulpit, or on the corner, speaking his mind. It is a man puttering in his garden in the evening, and swapping talk with his neighbor over the fence. It is the unafraid faces of men and women and children at the beach, or looking out of the car window speeding along a four-lane highway.*
It is a man saying, "Howdy, stranger," without looking cautiously over his shoulder. It is the people of the country making up their own minds. It is a ball game on a wonderful summer afternoon. It is a soprano singing "The Star-Spangled Banner" off key and meaning every word of it.
Freedom is the air you breathe and the sweat you sweat. It is you and millions like you with your chins up, daring anybody to take it away from you. 99

CHAPTER 7

A NEW BIRTH
OF FREEDOM

I am a great admirer of Abraham Lincoln. To me he is a hero. I look at his life and his words, and I invariably love my country more and strive a little harder to do all I can to support it.

The other night I sat and reread perhaps his most famous speech. It is only 226 words. There are but nine sentences. And yet, it is studied by patriots today as if it were new. I include it here to be read again and again. The temptation is to scan it quickly. We have all heard or read it many times. Many have memorized it. But read it slowly—carefully. It is one of the greatest speeches ever given. It was given at Gettysburg.

"Fourscore and seven years ago our fathers brought forth on this continent a new nation conceived in liberty and dedicated to the proposition that all men are created equal. Now we are engaged in a great civil war testing whether that nation, or any nation so conceived and so dedicated, can long endure. We are met on a great battlefield of that war. We have come to dedicate a portion of that field as a final resting place for those who here gave their lives that that nation might live. It is altogether fitting and proper that we should do this. But, in a larger sense, we cannot dedicate, we cannot consecrate, we cannot hallow this ground. The brave men, living and dead, who struggled here have consecrated it far above our poor power to add or detract. The world will little note nor long remember what we say here, but it can never forget what they did here. It is for us the living rather to be dedicated to the great task remaining before us— that from these honoured dead we take increased devotion—that we here highly resolve that these dead shall not have died in vain, that this nation under God shall have a new birth of freedom, and that government of the people, by the people, shall not perish from the earth."

Well, there it is—a masterpiece! I never fail to be impressed by its simplicity and its depth. I am always moved by its eloquence. But more than anything else, I am touched by the truthfulness of its message.

I believe that Abraham Lincoln's words need to be read in the halls of Congress, from the pulpits of America's churches, in the schools of our nation, and in the homes of our people. We need Lincoln's message as never before.

There is a phrase that we could well adopt as the theme of our nation this year and every year in the future. Listen again to Lincoln: "This nation under God shall have a new birth of freedom."

That is what we need: a new surge of freedom. This nation needs us to stand up and be counted. America needs loyal patriots to defend her from those within who would destroy her. We fool ourselves if we don't understand that there are men and women, American citizens, if you will, who are dedicated to her overthrow. It's time for you and me to take our places as defenders of this great nation.

I use an analogy of our present position as a nation. Do you remember hearing the account of a duck seen flying through the air with an arrow imbedded in its body? Well, not too long ago a picture appeared in a local newspaper and with it the story of a mallard duck who had eluded the attempts of rescuers to capture her and to remove the foreign object. A couple of months later a Canadian goose flew into Wisconsin with the same problem. A young bow hunter had hit his mark, but that didn't stop the bird. She had evaded game wardens, avoided tranquilizer-laced grain, and even dodged cannon-fired nets. Finally, after about a month, the wound seemed to exhaust the goose, and she was caught with a fishing net. Surgery was performed, and it wasn't long until she was returned to freedom.

Well, do you get the picture? If I'm not mistaken, if the signs are correct, America has sustained a wound or two in the last few years. These wounds weren't caused by Germany or Japan or Korea or Vietnam. They were self-inflicted. We have injured ourselves. Surgery is needed! And if we have the courage to perform that surgery, it won't be long until we, too, are flying high.

It's a little bit like my children. Every time they got ill, medicine was the solution. Now, ask me if my daughters wanted the medicine. You guessed it! Medicine just doesn't taste good. And how about slivers! Have you ever tried to remove a sliver from the hand of a child who pleads, throws up, screams, cries, and threatens to have God send several plagues upon your head? But the sliver must come out. And it isn't easy!

Lord Acton said, "Freedom does not consist in the right to do what we like, but in the right to be able to do what we ought." You and I have our freedom. So, the questions before us are: What ought we to do? What is the right thing to do? How should we operate? May I suggest a couple of things. They may be a little painful, but they'll put us back in working condition before long.

First, let's do what President Lincoln himself suggested. He counseled, "Stand with anybody that stands right and part with him when he goes wrong." It's about time we did that! You and I need to be tolerant but not go to the extreme. Right is right and wrong is wrong. We Americans have great patience with differing opinions. But enough is enough. The next time we see an injustice, let's say something. The next time we see the law broken, let's report it. The next time we're offered a chance to indulge ourselves, let's refuse.

As an example, a friend of mine recently went to the school board with a complaint about the permissiveness of his local high school. The outcome of his effort is still in doubt, but at least he went. Listen to what Thomas Paine has to say about people like my friend. "The summer soldier and sunshine patriot will, in this crisis, shrink from the service of his country; but he that stands it now, deserves the love and thanks of man and woman" (*The Crises, No. 1*). My friend is no sunshine patriot. And he deserves the thanks of every parent of every child in that school.

We don't need to be self-righteous about it. We don't need to be obnoxious. We don't need to be insensitive to those who differ in opinion. But America desperately needs us to stand up. It may even be a little embarrassing and, possibly, even a little painful. But stand we must.

Now, that's one thing we can do. Here's another:

Let me live in my house by the side of the road,
    Where the race of men go by—
They are good, they are bad, they are weak, they
    are strong,
    Wise, foolish—so am I.
Then why should I sit in the scorner's seat
Or hurl the cynic's ban?
Let me live in my house by the side of the road,
And be a friend of man.
(Sam Walter Foss, "The House by the Side of the Road," *The World's Great Religious Poetry,* ed. Caroline M. Hill [New York: Macmillan Co., 1923], p. 621.)

We need Americans to start caring about Americans. "Am I my brother's keeper?" Yes, I am!

I thought it would be appropriate if I used the president of the United States as an example. And since I love sports, I chose an incident from the young life of President Ronald Reagan. Here are the president's own words:

"Our football team stopped to spend the night in Dixon on our way to a nearby college where we were playing the next day. Coach Mac had told me that even though Dixon was my home, I'd have to stay with the team in the hotel. When we arrived, I went in the hotel with Mac to introduce him to the manager. To my awful embarrassment, I discovered that the hotel refused to admit my black teammates—our first-string center and reserve tackle—and that the other hotels in town also refused blacks.

"Mac was so mad he said we'd all sleep in the bus. As we started back to the bus, I said, 'Mac, won't it be embarrassing for Burky and Jim to know why we can't stay here?' He said, 'Well, what can we do?' I suggested that he tell the fellows we have to break up because the hotel can't take all of us, then put the three of us in a cab and we'd go to my house. That's what we did, and when my blessed mother opened the door, she didn't even blink. She just said with a big smile, 'Come right in.' " (*Parade Magazine,* June 29, 1986, p. 5.)

My, what we could accomplish if we would simply say, "Come right in." I don't mean that our homes have to literally be opened to every soul who passes our street (although I can still remember the special spirit of having our daughters' friends parade through our home; Grand Central Station had nothing on us). What I do mean is that Americans need to open their hearts, to feel and show tolerance, acceptance, compassion, and concern for their neighbors. If we could spiritually and emotionally say "Come right in," what a great boost for freedom this would be!

Daniel Webster once asked the significant question, "How much is all this worth?" What is the value of freedom? Is it worth the two suggestions I have made? That's just a start, but at least it is a start.

I know a man who has a beautiful Siberian Husky. The other day his dog tangled with a porcupine. Guess who lost? The dog's nose was full of porcupine quills. My friend was amazed as the dog stood quietly and allowed him to pull the quills out one by one. The dog cried a little each time one was removed, but he knew they needed to come out. He wanted them out!

Are there any quills or arrows that need removing in this great land? Are there changes that need to be made, painful or not? Do we have the courage to do what needs to be done? I think we do. My suggestions are simple, even though they may be difficult to implement at times, but if you and I will try them, our actions can make a difference.

Our efforts of strengthening and rebuilding freedom now will affect you and me and our children and grandchildren for years to come. It will mean the difference between continued freedom and dwindling opportunity. Eventually, it may make the difference between freedom and slavery, life or death. This is serious business!

Now, may we do what we know is right. May a new birth of freedom really come upon us. Then, like Andrew Jackson, we and our children can say, "Thank God my life has been spent in a land of liberty!" (Farewell Address.)

America's Defenders

" *America, we are thy sons*
And we shall keep thee free;
For in our veins there flows the blood
Of Washington and Lee.

No foreign flag upon thy sod
Shall we allow to stand;
No iron shackles from abroad
Shall touch thy foot or hand.

They mock thy army, say 'tis small
Thy navy, too, they scorn;
Have they forgot the laurels won
Since freedom here was born?

They say thy untrained citizens
Will never soldiers be;
Have they forgot those valiant men
Who fought in sixty-three?

America, thy sons are true
And if thou will but call
Ten million men will give to thee
Their homes, their lives, their all.

For thou dost stand for what is right,
For freedom of the seas;
God grant Old Glory may always float
Forever in the breeze. **"**

ANONYMOUS

CHAPTER 8

ON EAGLES' WINGS

Someone once said that tact is the art of building a fire under people without making them boil. I suppose after raising a family I ought to be able to do that.

It is wonderful to talk about the greatness of America. It is exciting to discuss the rededication of the Statue of Liberty. It is inspiring to talk of the freedoms we enjoy. But there is something else so significant about this great land that it must be mentioned. Without this "something," all the rest doesn't matter, because none of it will last unless we remember the charge. The Lord said, "For behold, this is a land which is choice above all other lands; wherefore he that doth possess it shall serve God or shall be swept off; for it is the everlasting decree of God" (Ether 2:10). Charles Kingsley said it in different words, "There will be no true freedom without virtue." Or, as a prophet has said, "Constitutional government, as designed by the framers, will survive only with a righteous people." (Ezra Taft Benson, *Ensign,* May 1976, p. 92.)

We can sing the national anthem until we are hoarse; we can pledge allegiance until our hands hang heavy; we can shed tears of joy over and over again as we watch our great United States athletes in the Olympics; but that is not enough. Our Heavenly Father, and every prophet he ever raised up, has proclaimed the truth in great simplicity: we either serve him righteously, or we won't last.

Allow me to heat the coals just a little. Recently I became aware, as did most of you, that Americans now consume 60 percent of the world's production of illegal drugs. That is incredible! There are twenty million regular users of marijuana. One hundred and fifty tons of cocaine will spread across this land during the next year. In other words, some four to eight million Americans will use cocaine; another half a million are heroin addicts. Nearly two thousand, mostly young adults, are arrested every day for drug crimes in the United States. In addition, we have over half a million of our citizens in prison; over one-third of them are there for drug-related crimes. Five thousand Americans alone die each year because of second-hand smoke. The statistics continue to increase.

Now, if that isn't enough to raise our anxiety for religious reasons, the social and physical problems certainly should. But whether we like it or not, the spiritual damage done to this great nation far outweighs that of any other nation. We cannot break the Lord's commandments and gain.

Let's turn up the heat. Think of the millions of abortions that are performed each year. Adultery is proclaimed as a way of life on the front pages of our "liberated" magazines. Homosexuality is condoned by millions of Americans, as well as by some religious groups of the land. America's doctors fear that forty thousand more Americans will be stricken with AIDS by 1988. And that list, also, continues to grow.

Then, did you know that this nation will probably raise the federal deficit ceiling to almost two and a half trillion dollars so that we can finance next year's looming budget deficit? That is another form of immorality. You and I get in trouble if we don't pay our utilities on time! And while we go further in debt, we spend more on public affairs than we do on drug enforcement.

I wish with all my heart that I could proclaim that "all is well in Zion." But it isn't.

Well, enough of the negative. We could preach calamity from here until doomsday. There are enough sobering facts to fill volumes. However, let's do become concerned. There certainly is a valid reason to be, and there is a way out.

Our generation isn't the first to be worried, however. General George Washington, even in his era, was troubled about the condition of our country. During the Revolutionary War he saw that "a decay of public virtue has fed the hopes of the enemy and kept the British arms in America to this day. They . . . declare this themselves, and add that we shall be our own conquerors. Cannot our common country, America, posses virtue enough to disappoint them?"

I believe that Washington's question could (and

should) be asked again today. "Cannot our common country, America, possess virtue enough to disappoint our enemies?"

I have an answer for that question. We can! It will take some time, but we can do it. And in the process of repenting, we can help those around us to do the same thing. We don't need to be preachy or overbearing. But we can set an example which will inspire those around us to follow our lead.

The spirit of righteousness I'm talking about is found in the following true story.

"A young boy went with his father, an American admiral in the early days of our history, down to New Orleans to quell a treasonable uprising created by Aaron Burr. The admiral's son, David, was about twelve years of age, and went as his cabin boy.

"Unwisely David took up smoking and swearing. His father worried. He was not a religious man, but he knew that those things would pollute that boy's life, especially while he was young. He, therefore, cautioned the sailors not to take David into their card games, and gambling, or to take him to the bar and treat him with liquor. David was learning to like the liquor, and learning also to like tobacco and swearing, and his father did not like that. He was a bright, active boy, and the sailors liked to have him in the game.

"Before they reached New Orleans the father decided there was only one thing to do and that was to get David to decide for himself.

"One day after the noon meal, the father dismissed the officers but said to David, 'Wait a minute.' After the officers passed to their various duties, the father shut the door and coming back to David, said: 'David, what do you intend to be when you grow up?'

"David threw back his shoulders: 'I intend to follow the sea!'

" 'Yes,' said the father, 'follow the sea. Be a poor miserable, drunken sailor, kicked and cuffed about before the mast, and die of fever in some foreign hospital.'

" 'No,' said David, 'I intend to tread the quarter deck and command as you do.'

"The father said, 'No, David, no boy ever trod the quarter-deck with such principles as you have, and such habits as you are exhibiting. You will have to change your whole course of life if you grow to be a man.'

"The father walked out and left David alone.

"As the prodigal son who ate husks with swine, also David came to himself. And he said, 'So that is my life, is it—to be a poor, miserable sailor kicked and cuffed about before the mast, die of fever in some foreign hospital? I'll change my life, and I'll change it now! I'll never drink another drop of intoxicating liquor—I'll never take the name of God in vain again— I'll never gamble!' And he walked out of the door.

"In about an hour, three sailors saw David pass, and said, 'Come here, and have a game of cards.'

" 'No, thank you,' said David.

"One said, 'What's eating the lad?'

"David went on, and then passed some who were drinking, who called out to him, 'Come have a drink, Dave.'

" 'No, thank you, I am not taking it any more.'

"A few said, 'Stay with it, lad.'

"And David did.

"The father quelled that treason of Aaron Burr. That is a matter of history, and then he returned home.

"Years afterward a banquet was given in a leading hotel in New York City in honor of an admiral who had won distinction in a recent war. He was the honored guest, and when the chairman arose to introduce him, he introduced admiral David Farragut of the United States Navy who, when he arose to acknowledge the welcome, said, 'Should you men like to know to what I owe my success in the Navy?' and a round of applause was the answer. And this was his response:

" 'It was all owing to a resolution I formed when I was a young boy, twelve years of age, acting as cabin boy to my father who went to New Orleans to quell the treason of Aaron Burr.' "

That's a marvelous testimony! Admiral Farragut gave us the key to the reestablishment of righteousness in this country. Let me repeat it: "It was all owing to a resolution I formed when I was a young boy."

Well, I continue to make resolutions, and I too resolve to try even harder to keep my life in order so that righteousness in our home can prevail, and I intend to encourage those around me to do the same.

If there were a great number of us who would join together in this resolution, imagine what we could do. Little by little, bit by bit, we could encourage righteousness among our people. After all, we have the Lord's promise if we do: "Righteousness exalteth a nation" (Proverbs 14:34). And where do we start? May I suggest that the basic Ten Commandments are still in vogue (see Exodus 20:1-17).

1. "Thou shalt have no other gods before me." (How about money? position?)
2. "Thou shalt not make unto thee any graven image." (How about cars? boats?)

3. "Thou shalt not take the name of the Lord thy God in vain." (How about T.V.? movies?)
4. "Remember the Sabbath day, to keep it holy." (How about worldly pursuits on this day?)
5. "Honor thy father and thy mother." (How about attitude? caring? helping?)
6. "Thou shalt not kill." (How about thought? intent?)
7. "Thou shalt not commit adultery." (How about infidelity? lust?)
8. "Thou shalt not steal." (How about improper "borrowing"? fraud? dishonesty?)
9. "Thou shalt not bear false witness." (How about rumors? gossip? white lies?)
10. "Thou shalt not covet." (How about jealousy? deceit?)

I believe that a resolution to more fully keep the Lord's Ten Commandments would make a great start in preserving this nation in righteousness. But it must begin with me! And then you! There is nothing wrong with cars and movies and golf if approached in the right way and with the right attitude. If we will place the Lord first, the rest will take care of itself. The drug problem will decrease; immorality will subside; family happiness will increase; personal satisfaction will grow. And, most important, the Lord will sustain us as a nation. Then our grandchildren will have a great future.

Our Heavenly Father spoke these words to ancient Israel: "Ye have seen what I did unto the Egyptians, and how I bare you on eagles' wings, and brought you unto myself. Now therefore, if ye will obey my voice indeed, and keep my covenant, then ye shall be a peculiar treasure unto me above all people." (Exodus 19:4–5.)

This nation cannot survive in unrighteousness! But if we all lend a hand, I bear witness that God will, in fact, bear us safely on eagles' wings.

I raise my voice in warning and encouragement with countless others who know, as I do, that God lives, that He is truly the Father of this land, and that we can begin to make a significant change for good. May we do so now and forever!

An American

" *I'm an American. Within my veins there flows*
The blood of all nations. Freedom is my birthright.
I know no fear of tyrant power or the sight
Of tinseled rank, among the rulers of the earth.
I tower, myself a king, son of patriot sires
And mothers who worshipped only God. I breathe
The air of liberty and know no law save right,
With love for God, and justice for my fellow man.
Yet unto the oppressed of every land and clime
I bring the fact of brotherhood and speak the joy
Of honest toil and educated mind. I rise
Upon the past; look not behind. I turn my eyes
Toward the sunrise of a new world with liberty,
Truth, and justice regnant among humanity. **"**

HORACE B. SELLERS

CHAPTER 9

THE AMERICAS— UNITED WE STAND

Recently, I read about an interesting experiment that was performed on two monkeys. Some scientists had devised a method of giving one of the monkeys "executive" training under carefully controlled laboratory conditions. The monkey chosen for training was strapped in a chair with his feet resting on a plate capable of giving him a minor electric shock. A light was put near him and was turned on twenty seconds before each shock. A lever was placed by the monkey's chair. If he pulled the lever immediately after the light came on, it would go out just as quickly and he would get no shock. It was amazing how fast he learned to avoid the shock.

The other monkey was placed across the room with the same setup, except that his lever didn't work.

However, both monkeys soon learned that the first monkey's lever would work for both, turning off the second monkey's light and protecting him from shock as well. This made the first monkey an executive, since he was now responsible for preventing the shock for the second one as well as for himself.

How interesting to think that monkeys can be trained to protect themselves and others. Now, I am sure you would agree with me that we humans are even more intelligent than monkeys. Occasionally, however, one could wonder how effectively man uses this wonderful intelligence he has.

In speaking of our world, General Omar N. Bradley once made a remarkably accurate and sobering statement about humans:

"With the monstrous weapons man already has, humanity is in danger of being trapped in this world by its moral adolescence. Our knowledge of science has clearly outstripped our capacity to control it.

"We have too many men of science; too few men of God. We have grasped the mystery of the atom and rejected the Sermon on the Mount. Man is stumbling blindly through a spiritual darkness while toying with the precarious secrets of life and death.

"The world has achieved brilliance without wisdom, power without conscience. Ours is a world of nuclear giants and ethical infants. We know more about war than we know about peace, more about killing than we know about living."

Well, maybe we're not as wise as we should be, but we mortals have great potential to help each other.

The willingness to help each other is one of the characteristics which has made America such a great nation. We have always been willing to join together to protect our sacred freedoms. We were even willing to fight together to establish our country. Our ancestors who signed the Declaration of Independence were English, Irish, Scottish, and Welsh. They were German, Dutch, Swedish, and French. They joined together in a great and glorious cause. And they were successful!

It is about such a cause that I have become increasingly concerned of late. In fact, it is impossible to talk of America without mentioning it.

Here is a great truth given to us by a prophet of God: "The whole of America is Zion itself, from north to south" (TPJS, p. 362).

That is quite a statement! Sometimes we become complacent as we consider the future of the United States. But the entire north and south continents of America belong together—they with us, we with them. We should not separate ourselves, physically or spiritually.

Speaking to an early-day prophet of this land, even before the birth of Christ, the Lord designated America in this way: "And this land shall be a land of liberty. . . . And I will fortify this land against all other nations. . . . Wherefore, I will consecrate this land. . . , for it is a choice land, saith God unto me, above all other lands." (2 Nephi 10:11, 12, 19.)

Well, that seems quite clear to me. But we have no idea where the prophet Jacob stood as he received that revelation from the Lord. Was it in what is now the United States? Chile? Colombia? Guatemala? Brazil? What we do know is that the Lord was not talking about a single country. He was speaking of a land! And that land is both North and South America.

So, may I suggest that as we consider the greatness and future of this nation, we add these names: Canada, Mexico, Guatemala, Honduras, Nicaragua, El Salvador, Costa Rica, Panama, Venezuela, Colombia, Ecuador, Peru, Bolivia, Chile, Guiana, Brazil, Argentina, Uruguay, and Paraguay. We do not stand alone. Neither do they. Together we form the promised land: "United we stand, divided we fall."

The United States fought for its independence from Great Britain. In the decade prior to the restoration of the gospel, many countries fought their own wars of independence. France, Spain, and Portugal all gave way to fledging nations in America. A great price was paid for the establishment of freedom throughout the continent. There is hardly a citizen of the United States who has not heard of George Washington or Thomas Jefferson. There is hardly a Latin who has not heard of Simon Bolivar. The Lord raised up great men throughout the land to establish it as Zion.

I believe that the United States has always been concerned, not only for herself, but also for the entire continent. It was that concern that brought forth from this nation's government a proclamation known as the Monroe Doctrine. Its central message is simple: "The American continents . . . are henceforth not to be considered as subjects for future colonization by any European powers." Joseph Fielding Smith said of that document:

"The greatest and most powerful fortification in America is the 'Monroe Doctrine.' . . . It was the inspiration of the Almighty which rested upon John Quincy Adams, Thomas Jefferson and other statesmen, and which finally found authoritative expression in the message of James Monroe to Congress in the year 1823." (*The Progress of Man* [Salt Lake City: Deseret Book Company, 1964], pp. 466–67.)

Since that time, our country has been increasingly concerned about the future of the entire continent. The problems of Nicaragua and El Salvador are critical to the future of this country. The problems of the United States are critical to Canada and Mexico. We are in this thing together.

Now, before we become self-centered in our concern for each other on this continent only, I submit that someday there must be a brotherhood of all nations if we are to survive. As people, we are not superior to the English, French, Danish, German, Egyptian, Israeli, South African, Japanese, Korean, or Chinese. We are all equally loved by a kind Father in Heaven. We Americans are privileged to live on this continent, but it is not because we are a superior people. It is simply because this land was preserved by the Lord for a specific and sacred purpose. But remember, "of him unto whom much is given much is required" (D&C 82:3). Our continent is a bastian of freedom to the world. Americans, both north and south, are to maintain that freedom for the sake of the world.

I read recently and was interested in some letters to the editor that were received from around the world as we celebrated the rededication of the Statue of Liberty. Let me share three:

"Congratulations, America, and happy birthday, Miss Liberty. America's democratic system is still the standard by which all others are to be judged." (The Rev. Gerald E. Curley, Toronto.)

"As a foreigner, I have concluded it is not only Americans who need America, the whole world does." (Frank Micallef, London.)

"For a great number of citizens of totalitarian and weak countries, the U.S. represents hope by defending freedom. I think every non-American has two fatherlands: his own and the U.S. I would be proud to be an American." (Jacky Chartin, Lorient, France. All three letters first published in *Time,* July 7, 1986, p. 9.)

As I have traveled the world, I have found a great empathy for the Americans, and vice versa. There are many who care. There must yet be many more.

This spirit of caring and concern is exemplified in a little story:

Once a king had a great highway built for the members of his kingdom. After it was completed, but before it was opened to the public, the king decided to have a contest. He invited as many as desired to participate. Their challenge was to see who could travel the highway best.

On the day of the contest the people came. Some of them had fine chariots, others had fine clothing, fine hairdos, or great food. Some young men came in their track clothes and ran along the highway. People traveled the highway all day, but each one, when he arrived at the end, complained to the king that there was a large pile of rocks and debris left on the road at one spot, and this got in their way and hindered their travel.

At the end of the day, a lone traveler crossed the finish line and wearily walked over to the king. He was tired and dirty, but he addressed the king with great respect and handed him a bag of gold. He explained, "I stopped along the way to clear away a pile of rocks and debris that was blocking the road. This bag of gold was under it all, and I want you to return it to its rightful owner."

The king replied, "You are the rightful owner."

The traveler replied, "Oh no, this is not mine. I've never known such money."

"Oh," said the king, "you've earned this gold, for you won the contest. He who travels the road best is he who makes the road smoother for those who will follow."

May I suggest that since we are all on the same highway, we might as well remove the obstacles from each other's paths. And above all, let us who live on this continent be sure we become an example of freedom to the rest of the world. To do so, we must truly become united. A modern prophet has put it perfectly:

"Today, we are in a battle for the bodies and souls of man. It is a battle between two opposing systems: freedom and slavery.

"I testify to you that God's hand has been in our destiny. I testify that freedom as we know it today is being threatened as never before in our history. I further witness that this land—the Americas—must be protected, its Constitution upheld, for this is a land foreordained to be the Zion of our God." (*Ensign,* November 1979, pp. 32–33.)

Let us unite, North and South America! Let us care about each other. There is no doubt in my mind that if we do, this continent will become the cradle of freedom God intended it to be. May it be so!

66 *We will walk on our own feet; we will work with our own hands; we will speak our own minds. The study of letters shall be no longer a name for pity, for doubt, and for sensual indulgence. The dread of man and the love of man shall be a wall of defense and a wreath of joy around all. A nation of men will for the first time exist because each believes himself inspired by the divine Soul which also inspires all men.* **99**

RALPH WALDO EMERSON

66 *What have you done for liberty? If nothing, what can freedom mean to you?* **99**

WILLIAM JENNINGS BRYAN

CHAPTER 10

AMERICA— THANK HEAVEN

Consider the following description of a truly remarkable person:

He hears an airplane overhead, and if he looks up at all, he does so in security, neither in fear nor in the hope of seeing a protector.

His wife goes marketing, and her purchases are limited by her needs, tastes, and budget, but not by decree.

He comes home on an evening through streets which are well lighted, not dimly lit in blue.

He reads his newspaper and knows that what it says is not concocted by a bureau, but is an honest, untrammeled effort to present the truth.

He adheres to a political party to the extent that he desires, and he reserves the right to criticize any of its policies—even if his convictions dictate that the theory of the country's government is wrong and should be scrapped.

He does not believe, if his party is out of power, that the only way in which it can come into power is through a bloody revolution.

He converses with friends, even with chance acquaintances, expressing freely his opinion on any subject, without fear.

He does not expect his mail to be opened between posting and receipt, nor his telephone to be tapped.

He changes his place of dwelling and does not report so doing to the police.

He has not registered with the police.

He carries an identification card only in case he should be the victim of a traffic accident.

He thinks of his neighbors across international borders as though they were across a state line, rather than as foreigners.

He worships God in the fashion of his choice, without fear.

He should struggle to preserve his Americanism with all its priceless privileges.

He is a fortunate man—he is *an American*. (Editorial in the *New York Sun*.)

Each one of us is also a very fortunate person. I, too, am a blessed man—thank heaven. Thank heaven for America! Despite our weaknesses, despite our problems, despite our challenges, this is the greatest nation on earth. As someone once said, "We haven't done badly for a nation of immigrants!"

But we haven't done it alone. We have done it because God helped us to do it. Our gratitude for America should be to Him. I think you'll remember with me George Washington's words at the conclusion of the convention at which the Constitution was adopted. He said:

"We have raised a standard to which the good and wise can repair; the event is in the hands of God. . . .

"Now, therefore I do recommend and assign Thursday the 26th of November next to be devoted by the people of these states to the service of that great and glorious being—who is the beneficent author of all the good that was, that is, or that will be—that we may then all unite in rendering unto Him our sincere and humble thanks. . . ."

That proclamation might very well be given 365 days of the year. How grateful we should be for this great land!

I thank heaven for the freedom we have in this country to enjoy the myriad of small, seemingly insignificant things that we so often take for granted. Just for a moment, look with me through the eyes of a marvelous Russian immigrant. Her name was Nila Magidoff and she married an American news correspondent who was working in Moscow. He was later forced to leave Russia, so the couple returned to his home in New York City. Let me relate just a paragraph from her story.

"One day, I took my first ride in the New York subway. I missed all my connections, not because of the movement of the trains, but because of the movement of many faces. It was then that I remembered the first time in my life I saw chewing gum. It was not in this New York subway. It was in the Moscow subway. Two beautiful American girls, tourists, were talking and chewing gum. Not one Russian moved from that train. When the Americans left, all the Russians left. Sitting next to me was an elderly Russian man. He looked at the girls and said, 'What a pity. Such beautiful girls and such a strange nervous disease.' "

Imagine any of us being thankful for gum! But there's a spirit in that little experience I hope you can feel.

Now, one more glance through Nila's eyes while she still lived in Russia:

"While I was waiting for permission to come to America, Robert went alone three times. I will never forget the excitement when he used to come back and bring with him all kinds of American gadgets. You see, you Americans don't know how much they meant, these 'little' things, to the Russian people, because there was always a shortage of consumer goods and because of our naive and childish curiosity for all kinds of gadgets.

"I remember once Robert brought an electric toaster. It was a toaster that everyone of you owned, that everyone of you use every day, but never notice. Not me! When I got a toaster, I telephoned all my Russian friends, 'Please come for American toast.' We put the toaster in the middle of the table. We put in two pieces of bread and waited without even breathing. You know, the bread 'jumped out' and then we put butter on it. Eight of us—we ate ten pounds of American toast!"

Chewing gum, toast, sugar cubes, popcorn, *Sports Illustrated,* hair dryers, Pampers, washing machines, TVs, cars, homes, families—we have so much. Thank heaven for America!

The spirit of gratitude that I wish we could all feel for this great land is illustrated by an experience I once had. During World War II, while I was serving in the infantry, I was engaged in a number of battles. During one of those campaigns on an island in the Pacific, my particular platoon drew the assignment to secure a military objective several miles into the jungle. On our reconnaissance, lo and behold, we came upon an enemy concentration camp. Incarcerated in this camp were some 2,500 to 3,000 natives. The enemy had abandoned the camp several minutes before, and I was honored to be one of the few soldiers to break down the barriers and bring freedom to this anxious group.

Words cannot describe the filth and misery that these people had experienced during their three years of imprisonment. Many children had been born under this extreme condition, and sickness and malnutrition were rampant. As we were hastily preparing to evacuate these unfortunate people to the beach area, I was standing inside the camp and was startled to feel a thump on my boot. Looking down in the mud, I found the form of a man who was perhaps in his sixties and who was barely recognizable as a living being. Upon examining him closer, I found that he was an American minister who had been trapped during the invasion and eventually taken prisoner by the enemy. Even though he was approximately six feet tall, he weighed less than one hundred pounds, and huge sores covered his body. As he struggled to gain some strength, his first request of me was, "Soldier, do you have an American flag?" I told him I did not have one with me, but I thought I could find one. After sending one of our jeep drivers to look for one, we prepared a stretcher, put him on it, and tried to bring the man as much physical comfort as possible under those conditions. We cleaned the mud from his face, gave him a drink of water, and administered minor first aid. When the flag was brought to us, I handed it to him. With tears in his eyes, he placed it over his bosom and said, "Thank God you have come!" In a very real sense, I, a nineteen-year-old soldier, saw in the face of a man who had experienced terrible tragedy the true meaning of freedom and of America. Thank heaven for America!

Now, my friends, let us not be ungrateful. In referring to the physical and spiritual blessings we enjoy in this land, the Lord has given us this counsel, which is scripture: "And in nothing doth man offend God, or against none is his wrath kindled, save those who confess not his hand in all things, and obey not his commandments." (D&C 59:21.)

We need to look around us and be thankful. As bad as our situation in this country sometimes looks, there is great hope if we give thanks to Him who is the giver of all our blessings. That gratitude and the accompanying determination to keep His commandments and live good and honest lives will see us through. I conclude with the words of a well-known hymn of praise.

> Our Fathers' God, to thee,
> Author of liberty,
> To thee we sing;
> Long may our land be bright
> With freedom's holy light.
> Protect us by thy might,
> Great God, our King!
> ("My Country, 'Tis of Thee,"
> *Hymns,* no. 339.)

May that prayer be answered upon this great land because of our righteousness as individuals and as a nation.

If we are to survive as an independent, sovereign nation, we must, as free Americans, follow sound economic and political policies, uphold and protect our constitution, and live to the letter the virtues of frugality, integrity, loyalty, patriotism, and morality.

EZRA TAFT BENSON

America became great not because of what the government did for the people but because of what the people did for themselves.

GEORGE W. ROMNEY

CHAPTER 11

GOVERNMENT
BY THE PEOPLE

One United States Senator asked his constituents what they thought were "the worst, most cumbersome, most senseless regulations imposed by the federal government?" And did he get an earful! His office was barraged with letters from within and without his state; it was the chance people had been waiting for. Griping about the government is fun, but official griping is all the better.

A small-town banker wrote that "it is time for Congress to give government back to the people." A CPA decried government as an "abominable paperwork monster."

Well, all of us like to sound off, but how many of us go any further than that? Most of us are guilty of walking into the voting booth and marking at least part of our ballots by guesswork. In fact, in most local elections it is almost predictable that the candidate whose name falls first in the alphabet and is thus probably first on the ballot will be the election winner. Can you imagine—government by alphabet soup? Heaven help the Zabriskie who wants to run for office.

Now, most of us have wonderful excuses for our poor citizenship. We'd like to get involved, to be informed, to make an impact on our world, but after all, we're too busy, right? It's so much easier to sit back and complain and wonder when "they" will do something about our beef. We're all too much like the man W. H. Auden describes in his poem "The Unknown Citizen."

The Unknown Citizen
(To JS/07/M/378 This Marble Monument Is Erected by the State)

He was found by the Bureau of Statistics to be
One against whom there was no official complaint,
And all the reports on his conduct agree
That, in the modern sense of an old-fashioned
    word, he was a saint,
For in everything he did he served the Greater
    Community.
Except for the War till the day he retired
He worked in a factory and never got fired,
But satisfied his employers, Fudge Motors Inc.
Yet he wasn't a scab or odd in his views,
For his Union reports that he paid his dues,
(Our report on his Union shows it was sound)
And our Social Psychology workers found
That he was popular with his mates and liked a
    drink.

The Press are convinced that he bought a paper
    every day
And that his reactions to advertisements were
    normal in every way.
Policies taken out in his name prove that he was
    fully insured.
And his Health-card shows he was once in
    hospital but left it cured.
Both Producers Research and High-Grade Living
    declare
He was fully sensible to the advantages of the
    Installment Plan
And had everything necessary to the Modern
    Man,
A phonograph, a radio, a car and a frigidaire.
Our researchers into Public Opinion are content
That he held the proper opinions for the time of
    year;
When there was peace, he was for peace; when
    there was war, he went.
He was married and added five children to the
    population,
Which our Eugenist says was the right number
    for a parent of his generation,
And our teachers report that he never interfered
    with their education.
Was he free? Was he happy? The question is
    absurd:
Had anything been wrong, we should certainly
    have heard.

(*The New Pocket Anthology of American Verse,*
ed. Oscar Williams [New York: World Pub. Co.,
1955], p. 62.)

What a perfect description Auden gives us of the average, sleepy citizen. So things in the society aren't always like you'd like them to be. "So what?" says the average man or woman, never thinking that their silence implies acquiescence. So there are others who may be working actively against the very kind of world you believe in. The quiet majority yawns, rolls over, and says, "Let me know how it all turns out." As another writer said, "More good things in life are lost by indifference than ever were lost by active hostility."

Some people like to use the excuse that their participation in society wouldn't matter anyway. They look at the masses and say, "I make no impact on society; I'm only a number. My voice and vote don't count." But consider this: In 1645 one vote gave Oliver Cromwell control of England. In 1776 one vote determined that English, not German, would be the American language. In 1923 one vote gave Hitler control of the Nazi Party. In 1941, two weeks before the bombing of Pearl Harbor, one vote saved selective service. These are only random instances in which one vote and one person made a difference.

Your voice can make an impact, too. In fact, if you'd lived in the Old West as a pioneer, you'd have hardly had the choice to stay on the fringes of community affairs. In the desert communities where water was as precious as gold dust, people's crops survived only through the extensive use of irrigation, bringing water from streams in nearby mountains. The rule was a simple one. If you didn't help build the irrigation system, your family didn't get any of the water it brought. That's what I call motivation. Instant community involvement. If you wanted your children to go to school and get an education, you paid the teacher personally, often in kind. The teacher might have received a chicken, a pound of wheat, anything an anxious parent could find to ensure his child's being taught. Such a system got a parent involved in schools and school policy quicker than any of today's homeroom mother assignments ever could. After all, he may have placed a chicken, let alone a child, on the line!

Well, where do you begin today to make an impact on a world that seems to get increasingly complex and removed from your touch? The place to begin is where you can have the most influence—in your own community, dealing with local problems. It is sometimes fun to imagine ourselves conferring with the country's president on some matter of national importance. We'd like to personally find a way to feed the world's starving millions. But in reality the world's gravest problems have their counterparts in our own communities. Crime, drugs, teen pregnancies, abused children —all of these are serious national problems with a need you can meet in your own area. As one political commentator advised, "Take a look at your community and find some project that needs doing. It may be removing a dead tree or there may be an empty house that should be torn down. Perhaps you have no library services, or the service available needs improvement. Maybe a stream is badly polluted or an industry pollutes the air. I don't care where you live; if you will sit down and start analyzing your community, you can come up with at least twenty projects which need doing."

In one small city, a group of citizens became concerned about the spread of pornography. More and more of what had been the better theaters in town were showing cheap X-rated movies. Supermarkets and other variety stores frequented by children displayed lewd magazines. It seemed that part of the downtown area was decaying morally and physically due to the theater clientele. Finally, just a handful of people went to local officials and asked that the laws regarding these establishments be carefully reviewed to see if they met community standards. The group presented careful arguments as to why there should be a city prosecutor who would concentrate on issues of pornography. They talked to managers in the stores they frequented to ask if certain kinds of material they considered offensive could be moved off open display. The result? The number of theaters in town showing pornographic movies was reduced from six to one. Throughout the area, stores cooperated by moving certain kinds of material off open display. It was only a handful of people who accomplished these things. But it was a handful of people who cared and who had done their homework so that they approached their goals rationally and not emotionally. It was a handful of people who were not afraid to get involved.

The Lord has said "that governments were instituted of God for the benefit of man; and that he holds men accountable for their acts in relation to them, both in making laws and administering them, for the good and safety of society" (D&C 134:1).

Whatever your particular political persuasion, whatever your concern, it is time now to let your voice be heard in the affairs of society. As Edmund Burke said, "All that is necessary for the triumph of evil is that good men do nothing." That we may all do "something" is my prayer.

" The condition upon which God has given liberty to man is eternal vigilance. "

JOHN P. CURRAN

" When a life of freedom becomes too difficult, when we fail to find joy in our own individuality, we surrender control to some organization which, as we think, has authority. It makes our important decisions for us. The freedom we then enjoy is the freedom of the slave. "

FROM *THE VAGABOND*

" There is a price tag on human liberty. That price is the willingness to assume the responsibilities of being free men. Payment of this price is a personal matter with each of us. To let others carry the responsibilities of freedom and the work and worry that accompany them—while we share only in the benefits— may be a very human impulse, but it is likely to be fatal. "

EUGENE HOLMAN

CHAPTER 12

AMERICA—THE GREAT AND BOLD IDEA

In May, 1950, a little girl named Dacey Eppermanis came to America. She was, only by chance, the one hundred and fifty thousandth refugee to arrive here after World War II. Because she represented the uncounted millions who had fled their countries and come here, a great celebration was held in her honor.

Hers was a story that had been repeated many times. Her home in Latvia had been overrun, first by the Russians, then by the Germans, and then by the Russians again. By some great fortune, her family's wartime wanderings placed her in Bavaria when peace came, not in the Russian occupation zone. After years of waiting, her family arrived in New York one Saturday morning.

Her speech at the celebration was a memorable

one. "May God help me," she said, "to find my place among the other children."

A quarter of a century later, another immigrant, a young boy named Robert Cousins, was one of a number of young people who came here one summer from Belfast, Ireland. His mother, though it had been difficult for her to do so, had sent him to this "far-away" place to get him away from an unhappy homeland. Inevitably, she regretted her decision and wrote for him to return, but he stayed. Robert's comments upon his arrival in America? "It's so good here," he said. "There's no shooting here, no bombs. I'm not scared." He is still here, now an avid supporter and defender of his adopted country and is a popular public speaker on many subjects across the nation, among them his love and appreciation for America.

Why do they come here, the Daceys and Roberts, the millions of men and women and children who sacrifice everything to try an alien land? Who are these "tired and poor, the huddled masses yearning to be free," who see such promise in America?

We who live here, who take so easily the blessings of freedom and liberty and equality, readily complain of our dissatisfactions. We grumble about high prices and smoky air, about injustices and poverty. And certainly many of our complaints and dissatisfactions are valid. But when we are tempted to look about us in anguish and despair, think about this:

When was the last time you heard a tank rumbling down your street?

When was the last time you had to go without buying a grocery item because of its scarcity?

When was the last time you paid $2.50 for a gallon of gasoline?

How long did your name have to be on a waiting list in order to find an apartment?

A Polish woman wrote this about America: "I love America because people accept me for what I am. They do not question my ancestry, my accent, my faith, my political beliefs. I love this country because when I want to move from one place to another I do not have to ask permission—I just go. I love America because I do not have to stand in line for hours to buy a piece of tough, fat meat. I love America because America trusts me. When I go into a shop to buy a pair of shoes, I am not asked to produce my identity card. My mail is not censored. My conversation with friends is not reported to the secret police."

She loves America, and we all do because this country was formed from a great idea, a really revolutionary idea in the history of man. You've heard this idea before. In Jefferson's immortal words it is this, "that all men are created equal, that they are endowed by their creator with certain inalienable rights." A government's basic role is to defend and protect those rights, not to frustrate, inhibit, or take them away.

Now the idea of equality among all men is an exalted one because everywhere we turn we seem to see nothing but evidences of inequality. Physically some men are three or four times as strong as others and are able to perform many times as much work. Intellectually the contrast is still greater, as may be realized when we compare someone like Albert Einstein with the average person on the street. And moral inequality is the greatest yet. The contrast between self-centered and cruel persons on the one hand and saints and heroes on the other cannot be measured.

"We can't even suggest that one man's opinion is as good as another's," said Elton Trueblood, a leading scholar. "If we were to take a million people at random and, on a question of astronomy, balance their judgment against that of six really skilled astronomers, possessing adequate instruments," he said, "it would be safer in case of conflict to trust the judgment of the six rather than the million."

With all these evidences of our inequality, it is a marvel that our government should recognize men as equal just because each is equally important in the eyes of God. It is a bold idea, an exalted idea that the uneducated and the university student are equally worthy of opportunity and consideration and justice before the law.

We do not live in a country that denies us our differences or refuses to admit that the best of us must be leaders. But we do live in a country in which each person has an equal chance to demonstrate whether he is one of the best.

And that is why the immigrants came. During the last century they came on ships, each carrying an exit pass, twenty-five dollars, and high hopes. Today there are millions more who would come if they could, all for the promise of vistas limited only by their own vision.

One woman who believed that the idea of patriotism was dead in her soul happened to be on a visit to Philadelphia. She decided that before she left, she would certainly have to see the Liberty Bell. It was a great effort for her to get to the spot. It involved subway rides and transfers, finding change and inconveniences.

At last she arrived and carefully made her way through the crowd so she could touch the bell. As she touched the cold metal, she had a mental vision of boys dying on battlefields for a great idea, of men and women braving a wilderness to test their fortitude, of two hundred years of belief that God made men equal, of a government that was no respecter of persons, of a constitution that was inspired.

And so she cried. Wet-faced she got back on her bus. A man, seeing her, asked with a heavy accent, "Why are you crying?" She quietly explained that she cried because she had touched the Liberty Bell. "You born in this country?" he asked.

She said, "Yes."

"Hey, you hear that?" the man yelled to everyone on the bus. "She was born in this country and she still understands."

There arose on the bus a great murmur about the woman who cried when she touched the Liberty Bell. A collection was taken up and with nickels and dimes and pennies the foreign-born Americans paid the bus fare of the woman who understood something about liberty.

America is a rich land with miles of fertile soil, virgin forests, and shining lakes. But the greatest wealth of our country is its varied, wonderful people— all so different, all equal because of a historic declaration. And whether we eat tacos, liverwurst, or lox and bagels; whether we are Polish, Spanish, or Chinese— being an American is a great gift.

Lyman Abbot once said, "A nation is made great, not by its fruitful acres, but by the men who cultivate them; not by its great forests, but by the men who use them; not by its mines, but by the men who build and run them. America was a great land when Columbus discovered it. Americans have made of it a great nation."

We may not be called upon to do something heroic in the name of democracy; we may not spend our days in flagwaving; but each of us in his own way can do his little bit to recognize the God-given equality of all men. We can love our neighbors on the wrong side of town; we can serve those who are different than we; and as we do we can sing with Walt Whitman, "Oh, America, because you build for mankind, I build for you."

With you I thank God for America, a land "choice above all other lands."

PART III

LET FREEDOM RING

AMERICA — A CHOICE LAND

What America Means to Me

66 *America is not just rich in material things, an industrial giant, a mighty military power. America is the country schoolhouse, the village church, the town meeting, the humble farmhouse, the rhythmic poetry of a peaceful countryside.*
America is the mirth and laughter of its children, the charity, the generosity, the compassion of its people. America is the triumph of merit and diligence over family and caste. America is the freedom of choice which God intended all men to have—the right to do, to speak, to worship, to dissent, to dream, to build, to fail and to succeed.
America is the marriage of liberty with authority, of individual freedom with social organization. America is the best discovery yet of a full and honorable way of life.
We are rich in all the things that decent people yearn for. It is our task to live up to these values and to make them known to every nation, friend or foe. For on us has fallen the challenge to lead the free. And the truth about ourselves is more powerful than any man-made missile. **99**

DEAN ALFANGE

CHAPTER 13

AWAKENING THE SLEEPING GIANT

Once in a while, a movie comes along that teaches an interesting lesson. There have been some in my lifetime. Because of my personal involvement in the Pacific Theater of war during World War II, I was quite interested to see the film *Tora! Tora! Tora!* The picture is about the attack by the Japanese on Pearl Harbor. One scene in the film shows a Japanese admiral standing on the deck of an aircraft carrier. The planes have already taken off for their attack. A radio message transmitted back to the bridge of the carrier reports that the bombing has commenced and that the United States has been caught sleeping and flat-footed. The admiral turns and looks out to the ocean and then, with a faraway look in his eyes, says: "I fear lest we have awakened a sleeping giant with a terrible resolve."

And awake we did! It took us from 1941 to 1945, but the giant awoke and he awoke with a "terrible resolve."

I firmly believe that the giant needs to be awakened again. I do not speak of a military awakening. We have considerable armaments. Our nuclear capacity seems to be sufficient. What I suggest is an awakening of all of us to a love and respect for this country of ours. Patriotism may seem to some to be outdated or used just for special occasions. But it will always be up-to-date to those who understand what this country is all about. It is somewhat frightening to see the military complex of America building both her offensive and defensive capacities, while some of her people seem to display disrespect towards the very things the military is committed to protect.

But I am an optimist. I believe that there are thousands upon thousands of patriots in our land who just need to be awakened. We need to rekindle the fire within each other. I am convinced that such an awakening can produce "a terrible resolve" in this country such as we have seldom experienced.

The kind of love and feeling for this country that I am speaking about is demonstrated in the great and old story of Philip Nolan, the "man without a country." It is a sad but heartwarming account of one man's discovery of America. I am convinced that every American ought to read or hear it often.

Philip Nolan had allowed his life to become entangled with the gifted and remarkable Aaron Burr. During the Revolutionary War, Burr had served his country well. But he was also an ambitious man. In a foolish, jealous challenge, he killed Alexander Hamilton in a duel. He lost the popularity he had previously held.

In his bitterness, Burr attempted to implement a plan to establish a new nation west of the Mississippi with himself as emperor. In 1795 he met Philip Nolan, a young officer in the American army. Nolan became fascinated with Burr and enlisted to help him in his cause.

Well, as you remember, the conspiracy was put down by the government and Philip Nolan stood trial for his treason. When Nolan was asked by the president of the court if he had anything to say for himself, the young, impetuous idealist shouted, "Damn the United States! I wish I may never hear the name of the United States again."

And, of course, he didn't. Young Nolan was taken to a United States armed boat and delivered to the naval commander with instructions that read something like this:

"You will receive from Lieutenant Neale the person of Philip Nolan, late a lieutenant in the United States Army.

"This person on his trial by court-martial expressed with an oath the wish that he might 'never hear of the United States again.'

"The court sentenced him to have his wish fulfilled.

"For the present, the execution of the order is intrusted by the President to this department.

"You will take the prisoner on board your ship, and keep him there with such precautions as shall prevent his escape.

"You will provide him with such quarters, rations,

and clothing as would be proper for an officer of his late rank, if he were a passenger on your vessel on the business of his Government.

"The gentlemen on board will make any arrangements agreeable to themselves regarding his society. He is to be exposed to no indignity of any kind, nor is he ever unnecessarily to be reminded that he is a prisoner.

"But under no circumstances is he ever to hear of his country, or to see any information regarding it; and you will specially caution all the officers under your command to take care that in the various indulgences which may be granted this rule, in which his punishment is involved, shall not be broken.

"It is the intention of the Government that he shall never again see the country which he has disowned. Before the end of your cruise you will receive orders which will give effect to this intention."

And so, for fifty-five years, Philip Nolan was never permitted to talk to anyone about this great land. He was allowed to read newspapers only after every reference to the United States was extracted. He never saw or heard mention made of America again until his death. He spent most of his time alone in his cabin.

But Philip Nolan did repent of his folly and accepted graciously the fate for which he had asked. He was nearly eighty years of age when he died at sea.

The first time the doctor entered his stateroom, Nolan was lying in his berth looking very frail. He smiled pleasantly as he gave the doctor his hand. As the doctor glanced around he saw the shrine that Nolan had made of his quarters. The Stars and Stripes were put above and around a picture of George Washington, and Nolan had painted a majestic eagle with its wings overshadowing the entire globe.

As the doctor was taking in the scene before him Nolan said, "Here, you see I have a country after all." Then he pointed to a great map of the United States that he had drawn from memory. He said, "Doctor, I know that I am dying. I have no home to go to. Surely you will tell me something about my country before I die." Seeing that the doctor was remembering the sentence, Nolan raised his hand and said, "Stop! Don't speak till I have said what I am sure you know, that there is not in this ship, that there is not in America— God bless her!—a more loyal man than I. There cannot be a man who loves the old flag as I do, or prays for it as I do, or hopes for it as I do. It has thirty-four stars in it now. I thank God for each one of them, though I do not know their names. I thank God that there has never been one star taken away. I thank God that there has never been a successful Aaron Burr. What a wretched dream to look back upon after such a life as mine."

"But," he said, "tell me, tell me something, tell me everything before I die." Then his guest said, "I will tell you everything you ask." A happy smile crept over Nolan's face, and he pressed the doctor's hand and said, "Tell me their names," and he pointed to the stars in the flag. Then the doctor told him the story of his country for those fifty-five long, lost years. He told him the story of immigration and steamboats and railroads and telegraphs and inventions and books and literature, of colleges and West Point, and of the Naval Academy.

Philip Nolan was a Robinson Crusoe, hearing for

the first time the answers to his accumulated questions of over a half a century. He was told the story of Abe Lincoln and how he had worked up through the ranks from a backwoods cabin. The tired old man drank in every word with unbelievable enjoyment. He said, "God bless Abraham Lincoln." Gradually Nolan became silent. Then he asked for the *Book of Public Prayer,* which lay close by, and with a smile he instructed his guest that it would open at the right place —and so it did, showing a double red mark running down the page. The doctor knelt down and read as they repeated together, "For ourselves and our country, Oh, gracious God, we thank thee, that notwithstanding our manifold transgressions of Thy holy laws, Thou has continued to us Thy marvelous kindness," and so on to the end of this psalm of thanksgiving.

Then together they repeated the more familiar words at the end of the book, saying, "Most heartily we beseech Thee with Thy favor to behold and bless Thy servant, the president of the United States, and all others in authority." Then Nolan said, "I have repeated those prayers night and morning; it is now fifty-five years." Then Nolan said that he would like to go to sleep. He was happy now and wanted to spend his last moments as he had spent most of his life, alone. He drew the doctor down and kissed him and said, "Look in my Bible when I am gone."

An hour later when the doctor quietly stepped back into his room, he found that Nolan had breathed his life away with a smile. On a slip of paper in the Bible Nolan had written this last request. It said:

"Bury me in the sea; it has been my home, and I love it. But won't some set up a stone in my memory at Fort Adams or at Orleans, that my disgrace may not be more than I ought to bear? Say on it,

In Memory of
Philip Nolan
Lieutenant in the Army of the United States.
He Loved His Country
As No Other Man Ever Loved Her;
But No One Deserved Less at Her Hands.

Well, I submit that if the feeling of love and patriotism engendered in the story of Philip Nolan could be awakened in us as a nation, we could accomplish everything. Everything!

The question is: "How do we awaken the sleeping patriots of this nation?" I remember while serving as a mission president that I had several missionaries who had to be awakened each morning with "sticks of dynamite"!

I believe that Philip Nolan himself left the keys to the awakening of this giant of America. On one occasion, while talking with a young man on board his ship, Nolan gave some advice that needs to be read in every home and school of this nation:

"Young man, . . . if you are ever tempted to say a word or do a thing that shall put a bar between you and your family, your home, or your country, pray that God in His mercy will take you home to His own heaven that instant. Stick by your family, boy; . . . think of your home, boy; write and send and talk about it. Let it be nearer and nearer to your thought, the farther you have to travel from it. And when you are free, rush back to it. . . . No matter what happens to you, no matter who flatters you or who abuses you, never look at other flags, never let a night pass but that you pray to God to bless that flag. Remember, boy, that behind the men, behind the officers, the government, and even the people, there is the country itself, your country, and that you belong to her as you belong to your own mother. . . . Oh, if someone had said that to me when I was at your age!" (Edward Hale, *The Man Without a Country* [Boston: Roberts Brothers, 1897] pp. 30–32, 88–91.)

Philip Nolan suggested at least four "sticks of dynamite" which will awaken us all:

1. Let us stop the negative criticism of America that goes on so frequently and instead find the good that is all around us. Let's stick up for her every chance we get.

2. Let us talk of and write about and keep in our thoughts the blessing of being an American. Why not refer to America in our conversation and habits? Why not write of it in our letters? Why not consciously think of her in our daily lives?

3. Let us honor the flag. Why not buy one and keep it where we can use and see it? It's pretty difficult to put up and take down the "Stars and Stripes" and not consciously think of America.

4. Let us talk of America in our homes and share our pride with our children. The younger generation needs to know how we feel about this land. I think they would be amazed at the depth of the feelings of most of us about this country. Our young people in

particular need to know of our love for and commitment to America.

Now, can you imagine the explosion and reawakening that would occur in America if we took Philip Nolan's simple advice? I suppose that desire in me is one reason for this book.

God bless America! May He help us to rekindle our "terrible resolve." May He help us to do something about what has been written. May God help us to awaken!

  ❝ *We still have it in our power to rise above the fears, imagined and real, and to shoulder the great burdens which destiny has placed upon us.* ❞

HELEN KELLER

  ❝ *True patriotism sometimes requires of men to act exactly contrary, at one period, to that which it does at another, and the motive which impels them—the desire to do right—is precisely the same. The circumstances which govern their actions change; and their conduct must conform to the new order of things.* ❞

ROBERT E. LEE

  ❝ *Freedom is not free. It has to be nourished with each new generation—worked for, fought for, and sometimes died for.* ❞

KARL PRUSSIAN

CHAPTER 14

MORE THAN
A MELTING POT

There is a great tradition surrounding the Statue of Liberty. To all immigrants who come to the United States of America through New York Harbor, she represents the opportunity to make a new life for themselves—and rightfully so!

We are all familiar with the term *melting pot*, which, in reference to the makeup of our society, means that many nations, kindreds, tongues, and people have come together to form a nation of immigrants. The only people who are not foreigners are the American Indians.

But I believe that America is much more than a melting pot, much more than just bringing people together. First of all, when many ingredients are put together and mixed, they become blended in such a way that there is a "sameness," that each loses its own characteristics. For example, putting strawberries, peaches, milk, and sugar in a blender and mixing well results not only in a delicious drink but also in a mixture that looks very uniform in each glassful. Where Americans are concerned as we are all brought together, a certain sameness or blending of some of our values, philosophies, traditions, even customs is desirable, but it is also extremely important that each of us retains his own individuality, his own personality traits, habits, goals, talents, gifts, and even his culture.

Second, in the American ideal, *melting pot* denotes to me the chance to progress, the freedom to succeed.

In these United States, then, where there is a mixture of many nationalities and where individual differences exist, not only naturally but desirably so, as surely as the sun rises, so do some of us. Cream rises to the top and ice comes to the surface of the water. And America allows those who have the initiative to rise to the top of the melting pot.

Here's an example of that very principle. In July 1986 the nation celebrated the relighting of the Statue of Liberty. What a great sight that was! And on Governor's Island, in conjunction with the rededication of Miss Liberty, twelve naturalized citizens were honored with the Medal of Freedom. These twelve were chosen for their contributions to this country. They are worth mentioning:

1. Irving Berlin, Russian-born composer. Have you heard "God Bless America" lately? That was one of his!

2. Franklin R. Chang-Dias, born in Costa Rica. Do you remember him? He was the first Hispanic-

American to orbit the earth aboard the shuttle Columbia.

3. Kenneth B. Clark, Jamaican-born psychologist. His work on the problem of blacks in America was cited by the Supreme Court in 1954 when public school segregation was declared unconstitutional.

4. Hanna Holborn Gray, born in Germany. She is the dean of the University of Chicago, the first woman to hold the executive office of a major American coed school of higher learning.

5. James B. Reston, native of Scotland. Have you read any of his work lately? He's a Pulitzer Prize– winning columnist with the *New York Times.*

6. Bob Hope. Did you know that Bob was born in England? Is there anyone in the free world who hasn't been affected by his marvelous humor?

7. Henry A. Kissinger, German born. You may not always agree with his politics, but as Secretary of State, he accomplished some wonderful things.

8. I. M. Pei, a native of China. If you've been to New York, you've seen products of his architectural genius, including the Robert Kennedy Memorial and the Javits Convention Center.

9. Itzhak Perlman, Israeli violinist. You may or may not like classical music, but you have to stand in awe of his great gifts and talents.

10. Albert B. Sabin, from Poland. Next time you or your children take polio vaccine, say a word of thanks for Dr. Sabin.

11. An Wang, Chinese born. My secretary types on a computer made by his company. She makes me look good! Thanks, Mr. Wang!

12. Elie Weisel, Romanian. He is a superb writer and philosopher. You may have read one of his many works.

Well, there we have it. Twelve men and women who have risen to the top of the melting pot. Not bad for a group of immigrants! Having freedom is one thing, but doing something with it is another. These twelve did something with it.

Have you ever noticed that the beautiful lady on Ellis Island doesn't guarantee success? She'll put us in the pot, but it's up to us to rise to the top. It takes effort, sometimes even against overwhelming odds, but it can be done. Let me illustrate:

"Scientists believe that millions of years ago the earth was covered by a luxurious vegetation far more dense than that found in today's densest jungles. During one of the great upheavals which occurred in this period, the earth sank in certain places and the vegetation was covered with mud and water and subjected to great temperature and pressures.

"This vegetation then became *peat.* Peat bogs are found in Pennsylvania, Michigan, and Wisconsin in this country and in Ireland. Peat will burn, but with a smoky flame and low fuel value.

"Additional pressure will convert the peat into *lignite,* which is sometimes called brown coal, and which has slightly more fuel value than peat.

"Further pressure results in the formation of soft or *bituminous* coal. This has a higher percentage of carbon and a still greater heat value than lignite.

"*Anthracite,* or hard coal, comes only with considerably more pressure. It has the highest percentage of carbon and the greatest heat value per pound, and burns with a clean, hot, long-lasting flame. It is more expensive, but also more desirable than the other fuels.

"The ultimate in carbon deposits, however, is the *diamond,* a form of *pure* carbon. Diamonds result from *extreme* pressure on *pure* carbon in nature. The finest of all diamonds is the blue-white diamond.

"In all of these carbon substances, the difference in value is the degree of pressure to which they have been subjected.

"The more pressure they have withstood, the harder they become!" (Lindsay R. Curtis, *Talks That Teach* [Salt Lake City: Bookcraft, 1963], pp. 76, 78.)

I believe that freedom is a matter of not only being thrown in the melting pot, but also of doing something about it, not just blending but rising to the top. And then, of course, we can allow those around us the opportunity to do the same. An anonymous, wealthy philanthropist from New York did that very thing for his son. He said:

"As I get older and think of my only son, I don't want to leave him a big fortune, just enough to keep the wolf away. He doesn't deserve millions; it would do him more harm than good. I prefer to leave the money to eleemosynary institutions [those supported by charity] to benefit mankind. I've had lots of fun making money, and now it must go back to the people it came from."

How's that for a caring parent? He simply threw his son into the melting pot. May I be truthful? I thought of doing the same thing to my three daughters when they were teenagers. I did, in a way, and it is a blessing to see them succeed on their own.

Well, the opportunity to rise is ever present. But so

is the opposite. Miss Liberty can only do so much. The rest is up to you and me. I remember a chaplain at one of our state penitentiaries who said:

"I have talked to many men in prison before they go before the Board of Pardons to ask for their freedom. I have asked some the question, 'Do you want to be released? Do you want to go back into society?'

"They look at me as much as to say, 'What a stupid question; of course we want to get out of here.'

"Then I ask, 'Are you willing to do your share of the world's work, care for yourself and others dependent upon you for a livelihood? Or are you one who thinks the world owes you a living? If so, this is the place to collect it: food, clothing, shelter, leisure time, recreation and no expense. The state will even take care of your family. The decision is yours.' " (Ray F. Smith, "The Decision Is Ours," *Instructor,* Nov. 1959, p. 360. Used by permission.)

Anyone who decides to rise to the top can do it. But freedom also allows the opposite. We can lie on the bottom and let life pass us by. We can let others take care of us. We can settle for mediocrity. We can rebel. Patrick Henry said: "The shepherd drives the wolf from the sheep's throat, for which the sheep thanks the shepherd as his liberator, while the wolf denounces him for the same act."

You and I can be thankful for our freedom as we do something about it. Or we can dislike those who try to help us understand freedom. Being thrown into the liberty of a melting pot sometimes hurts (you should have heard me scream when my dad insisted I get in), but there is no other way for growth. Freedom and growth must exist together!

Now, to conclude, let's put things in perspective:
1. The melting pot is America.
2. We can rise to the top by the wise use of our freedom.
3. Such a course is not easy.
4. Great men and women continue to do it.

Yes, millions of Americans have risen to the top. Success, however, is not measured by the Medal of Liberty or by the honors of men. The twelve Americans honored by this country are representative of the greatness of thousands. Included in those rising to the top are children, teenagers (that's right, even teenagers), moms and dads, brothers and sisters, men and women, blacks and whites, the normal and the "handicapped." These, our brothers and sisters, quietly use their freedom to improve themselves and those around them. Perhaps none will have the occasion to give a "Patrick Henry talk." But, in their own way, they contribute just as much to the greatness of this land.

God has given us our freedom. He created the melting pot in which we can thrash around and rise. What a great combination! What a great opportunity! May you and I use it. May we take our freedom and, by hard work, lift ourselves and all those around us. May this country be, truly, more than just a melting pot—may it be God's light of freedom to all the world!

" My country owes me no debt. It gave me, as it gives every boy and girl, a chance. It gave me schooling, independence of action, opportunity for service and honor. In no other land could a boy from a country home without inheritance or influential friends, look forward with unbounded hope. "

HERBERT HOOVER

*" To play my role with a heart that sings,
To know the richness of simple things,
To feel I've paid for what I've won,
In the honest coinage of duty done;
To seek the weal of our brotherhood,
And share in the larger common good,
To keep the faith with my race and day—
That's what I call the American Way. "*

JOEL D. SMITH

CHAPTER 15

THE BRAVERY
OF BROTHERHOOD

As I have frequently and proudly stated, I love America! Together with thousands of veterans from several wars I have had the privilege of defending this great country. You can't go through such experiences without some pretty strong feelings about this land. I have seen men rise above their own fears and perform great acts of courage. Words like *bravery* and *courage* took on new meaning for me while as a nineteen-year-old boy, I was exposed to the reality of battle.

With that thought in mind, I listened with great interest when the president of the United States spoke at the Statue of Liberty centennial celebration. He made a statement that has made a deep impression on my soul. In speaking of the physical courage demonstrated over and over again in defense of this nation,

President Reagan called for a different kind of bravery —a bravery needed particularly in our day and age, a bravery needed on a different kind of battlefield. He called it the "bravery of brotherhood."

Courage to stand in hand-to-hand combat with an enemy is one thing, but taking an enemy by the hand is quite another. It is sometimes easier to fight a brother than it is to be one. But such an act is what America is all about—brotherhood! Dr. David Hyatt, President of the National Conference of Christians and Jews, spoke of the great need for brotherhood. He said, "Brotherhood is democracy at work! It is giving to others the rights and respect we want for ourselves. It can be that simple and that profound." (NCCT pamphlet, Dec. 1974, p. 3.)

That's a pretty simple definition of brotherhood. That's my kind of definition! The Lord put it only a little differently: "Therefore all things whatsoever ye would that men should do to you, do ye even so to them" (Matthew 7:12).

I guess what brotherhood is all about is treating one another like brothers, treating others like we would want to be treated. It isn't easy, but it's what makes America the great nation she is. It separates us from all the other countries.

I believe that brotherhood is possible! It is certainly needed! And it is needed now!

The spirit of the brotherhood I'm talking about is demonstrated so well in a true story told by a good friend and former colleague of mine. He relates:

"It was during World War I. We had a man in our regiment who was as tough as any man in the regiment; He was known as the unsentimental cuss; he was the kind of man that nobody liked. We thought he had no sense of emotion or of sympathy or of understanding, that he could see his comrades shot down by his side and never bat an eye, and we didn't think he had in him anything that would indicate that he had any sentiment at all. I was guilty of saying in my heart, though I didn't speak it out loud, 'I thank thee, God, that I am not like that man.' [See Luke 18:11.] There was another Pharisee once who said that, and this time I was the Pharisee.

"We were in France. This man was called on duty to examine the mail, incoming and outgoing mail. [That is quite an interesting job; you read some very interesting letters. For instance, I remember reading a letter from a young fellow to his girl, undoubtedly very sincere, in which he told her of the good time he was having and how he missed her and how he loved her. Then he must have been called suddenly to duty, because he said, 'I am feeling fine, but I am as lousy as a pet coon.' And then underneath he scribbled, 'Hoping this finds you the same.']

"Well, this unsentimental cuss was on duty reading mail, and he read a certain letter, a letter from Mrs. Jock Anderson out in London, Ontario, Canada. She was writing to her beloved Jock, and she said to him: 'We are getting on all right, my dear. The ten little bairns are coming along. I have had to wean the baby because I have to work to support the others, but we are mighty proud of you and proud of where you are. But, Jock, dear, our neighbor three months ago received word that her husband was missing. She said she had rather heard he was dead—she said she could hardly stand the uncertainty of it.' Then she added, 'Jock, my dear, join with me and pray God that I may never get word that you are missing.'

"This unsentimental officer read that letter but said nothing about it. That night there was paraded before him a sergeant and six men who were going out into no-man's-land. They called the roll; the officer heard the name Jock Anderson among those who were going out. They went out, and in the morning the sergeant and three men came back. Again they called the roll, and Jock Anderson did not answer. The officer said to the sergeant, 'Do you know where Jock Anderson fell?'

"The sergeant replied, 'Yes sir, he fell on an elevation on which is trained the enemy's machine gun.'

"The officer asked, 'Do you think a man could go out to that body and get the identification disc off his neck?'

"To which the sergeant answered, 'Sir, it would be absolute suicide, but if you say so I will try.'

"Then the officer said, 'I didn't mean that, I just wanted to know.'

"[You know, in World War I you could not declare a man dead unless his body or his identification disc could be produced.] That night that unsentimental officer was missing. And the next morning there came up to the front lines a large regimental envelope. When it was opened there fell out an identification disc with the name of Jock Anderson on it and a short note that said, 'Dear Major: I am enclosing the identification disc of Jock Anderson. Please write to Mrs. Anderson in London, Ontario, Canada and tell her God heard her prayer—her husband is not missing.'

"That was the man of whom I had said, 'I thank thee, God, that I am not like him.' He had the courage which I never had to crawl out on his stomach in the face of almost certain death in order to bring to a woman he had never seen, three thousand miles away, the poor comfort that her husband was not missing.

"And on the bottom of his letter he wrote, as though it didn't amount to much, 'As for me, I am off for Blighty in the morning. The doctor says it is an amputation case and may prove fatal. Cheerio.' " (Hugh B. Brown, *The Abundant Life* [Salt Lake City: Bookcraft, 1965], pp. 128–30.)

Now, what we have here is much more than physical courage. Much more! We have the bravery of brotherhood in its finest sense. I have met men like the officer descibed by my friend. That kind of person may be a little blustery on the outside, but he knows what it means to treat others as he would want to be treated.

Let's take brotherhood one step further. The Lord put the challenge in these words: "And he inviteth them all to come unto him and partake of his goodness; and he denieth none that come unto him, black and white, bond and free, male and female; and he remembereth the heathen; and all are alike unto God, both Jew and Gentile." (2 Nephi 26:33.)

May I be so bold as to assume that none of us has yet perfected our ability to demonstrate the kind of brotherhood talked about by the Lord? But there are many who are working on it. What our nation needs is more to join in the effort. The more that do, the greater America will become.

I remember reading of a young school boy who learned the meaning of the bravery of brotherhood. During World War II this boy had heard all the "appropriate" words: *Japs, Yellowbellies, Krauts, Wops,* and so on. In addition he had heard of some of the places: Pearl Harbor, the Philippines, Okinawa. He knew that "Japs" were yellow and to be hated. One day his friend came to school with the "good" news that his uncle had killed a "Jap" and had sent the souvenirs home. They were going to be displayed Friday in school. But thank God for a sensitive, wise teacher. On the appointed day, the souvenirs were all on the table: a flag, an ammo belt, and a bayonet. The students could all picture how the uncle had killed to get these things. But then the teacher did something that changed the meaning of brotherhood for her class—forever. After the excitement of the souvenirs had subsided, the teacher spoke. Let's listen to the rest of the story in the boy's own words.

" 'Here is one souvenir you haven't seen yet.' said Mrs. Ricketts as she unwrapped a scarf and placed a bamboo-designed wallet on the table. As I opened it up I stared in disbelief. There across from his identification information was a picture of a handsome Japanese man, a pretty wife, and five children. One girl and four boys, exactly like our family. We had just had a family picture taken, and [the Japanese family was] even standing like we had stood. I couldn't take my eyes off the man; he looked like my dad and combed his jet-black hair back the same way my dad did.

"The most terrible and frustrating feeling passed over me as I stood frozen with that wallet in my hand. I suddenly felt very uneasy and for days following was depressed to think that someone just like my father had been killed. I would look at Dad as he sat at the table or as we went fishing, to work, or to a Roy Rogers show and would always think of the enemy father and his boys. I tried to avoid projecting myself into the position of the enemy's son, but I couldn't help it. The experience remained with me and haunted me for years because Mrs. Ricketts had pointed out that the soldier had been a loyal man, a grocer, and was just like all of us; his country was our enemy, but he wasn't.

"Due to my limited rural exposure, I never really knew a Japanese or German while I was growing up. I pitched baseball against one Japanese boy in high school and occasionally ate at a cafe that his parents operated, but throughout high school I still housed the propaganda, the frustration, and the confused compassion within me.

"At nineteen I found the Church, and one year later, following some intense preparation and involvement, I accepted a mission call to the Hawaiian Islands. When I arrived there, I found that the majority of the population was Oriental, and upon hearing words like *Pearl Harbor* and *Honolulu,* many childhood war memories which I thought I had forgotten were aroused again.

"The first night out in the tracting area, we were invited after a day's work to have supper at the bishop's house. When the bishop opened the door I almost gasped. He was Japanese!

" 'A Japanese bishop?' I thought. 'How could it be?' But it was. He was a sharp UCLA graduate, and when he talked to us . . . that evening, tears rolled out of those almond-shaped eyes as he fervently testified of his love and commitment to the Prophet Joseph Smith and to President McKay. All of my frustrations of childhood and teenage years suddenly came into focus as I felt a deep warmth and love for that young bishop. He became, in my own mind, the father in the picture in the dead soldier's wallet. I left his home that evening relieved of a burden I had carried for fourteen years, and I left with a commitment to maintain and expand that warm spirit of kinship which I had experienced while listening to the testimony of the Japanese bishop." (Don Aslett, "My Souvenirs from World War II," *Ensign,* July 1978, pp. 25–26. Used by permission.)

What a marvelous experience! Imagine what could happen to our nation if we could learn to be brothers. I often wondered, as I sat in distant foxholes, what the world would be like if all nations had the gospel.

One of the great miracles of this country is the fact that we have been able to grow together—blacks, whites, Orientals, Indians, English, French, Danish, Spanish, and so many others—we are here together. We work together, we play together, we worship together, but the miracle can become even more powerful as we include everyone in it: the poor, the handicapped, the underprivileged. There is room for everyone; there is growth available to all.

The story is told of a boy who was extended an invitation to visit his lumberjack uncle up in the Northwest.

"[As he arrived] his uncle met him at the depot, and as the two pursued their way to the lumber camp, the boy was impressed by the enormous size of the trees on every hand. There was a gigantic tree which he observed standing all alone on the top of a small hill. The boy, full of awe, called out excitedly: 'Uncle George, look at that big tree! It will make a lot of good lumber, won't it?'

"Uncle George slowly shook his head, then replied, 'No, son, that tree will not make a lot of good lumber. It might make a *lot* of lumber but not a lot of *good* lumber. When a tree grows off by itself, too many branches grow on it. Those branches produce knots when the tree is cut into lumber. The best lumber comes from trees that grow together in groves. The trees also grow taller and straighter when they grow together.' " (Henry D. Taylor, in Conference Report, Apr. 1965, pp. 54–55. Used by permission.)

This nation was founded on the belief that we can all grow together. But it takes courage to reach out to those around us; the unknown is always a bit scary. But we are needed. You need me and I need you. There are thousands who silently cry out for the brotherhood of those around them.

Why don't you and I rededicate ourselves to each other? to those around us? Why don't we decide that the great principle of brotherhood upon which this nation was founded will be strengthened by our own small contribution? Friendship, caring, brotherhood— they all go together. They take bravery—the bravery to overcome our own insecurities and reach out. We can do it!

> America! America!
> God shed his grace on thee,
> And crown thy good with brotherhood
> From sea to shining sea.
>   (*Hymns,* no. 338.)

May that be so! May we have the courage to extend our brotherhood from one end of this nation to the other. Such action made America great—such action will keep her great!

"Freedom of thought, freedom of speech, freedom of action within the boundaries that do not infringe upon the liberty of others are man's inherent rights, granted him by his creator."

DAVID O. MCKAY

"Our defense is the spirit which prizes liberty as the heritage of all men in all lands everywhere. Destroy this spirit, and we have planted the seeds of despotism."

ABRAHAM LINCOLN

"The destiny of any nation at any given time depends on the opinion of its young men under twenty-five."

CHAPTER 16

"GIVE ME LIBERTY"

I sat in a small park the other day. The sun was bright. A few bright puffy clouds drifted lazily overhead. The grass was green and some rose bushes were bright with flowers. There was a gentle breeze.

As I sat and watched my grandchildren, together with some youngsters from around the park, I was moved. They laughed; they giggled; they played; they ran. The day was beautiful and so were they. And as I sat there and watched those tots, I wished it would never end. Where else in the world could children be quite as free to run and play as in that park? In the USA? And then, because of my experience with war I suppose, I wondered if it could ever end. And a thought down deep came, "Give me liberty. . . ."

I walked across a beautiful college campus the other day. The students wore Levi's and T-shirts. They carried backpacks full of books. They went to class (at least on occasion), and if they didn't like what the professor said, all they had to do was raise their hands and disagree. I loved watching those young Americans. I guess I'm getting a little sentimental as I get more mature, but I was moved! And once again I wondered if it could end. And again the thought came, "Give me liberty . . ."

I was recently invited to take a tour of a printing plant. The presses were gigantic. (I think my grandkids would call them "awesome.") I was impressed. But the most impressive of all were the people who worked there. They were of all ages. Some were white, some were black. Some were male and some female. Hispanics were there, as were several nationalities I couldn't specifically identify. One mentally handicapped boy swept the floors. Each took pride in his work and they all earned a wage. For some teenagers, it was a minimum wage. For some of the technicians, much more. But they all had the freedom to apply themselves. They could all quit if they wanted to. They were there because they wanted to be. They were free! Once again, I was moved. And, once again, I wondered if it could end. And the thought came, "Give me liberty. . ."

I sat in the stands at a baseball game on a recent day off and watched a great game. I really got "into it." We were jammed in everywhere: kids, moms and dads, businessmen, teachers, gas station attendants, bankers, old fans and young. We were there to enjoy a game and root for the home team. As we sang "The Star-Spangled Banner" I got a lump in my throat. And one more time I wondered if it could ever end. Could there be a life without hot dogs and pop? And again from down deep in my heart came the thought, "Give me liberty. . ."

Well, I think it's only right to finish the statement that I keep referring to. You all know it; some by heart. Patrick Henry gave a powerful speech just before the signing of the Declaration of Independence. And these are his words:

"Is life so dear or peace so sweet as to be purchased at the price of chains and slavery? Forbid it, Almighty God! I know not [the] course others may take, but as for me, give me liberty or give me death!"

Children playing in the park; students walking across the campus; factory workers on the job; fans eating hot dogs at a game; and again the question comes: Could it all end?

Abraham Lincoln was once asked, "What constitutes the bulwarks of our liberty and independence?" He replied, "It is not our frowning battlements, or bristling sea coasts, our army and navy . . . , our reliance is in the love of liberty which God has planted in us."

Well, God certainly planted liberty in me! I love to look at "Old Glory" and sing hymns of praise to America. There isn't much I do that makes me happier. Some Americans feel as I do, some don't.

I have to smile when I make that statement, because some change their minds as circumstances change. I am reminded of a little anecdote about such a person:

"A woman was being examined in court for jury service. 'I'm sorry, Your Honor,' she told the judge, 'but I can't serve on this jury. You see, I'm against capital punishment.'

" 'Maybe you don't understand,' the judge told

her. 'This is a civil suit brought by a wife to recover five thousand dollars of *her* money spent by her husband on gambling and on other women.'

" 'Oh,' said the woman, 'in that case I'd be happy to serve on the jury. I could be wrong about capital punishment!' " (*Bits and Pieces,* May 1968, p. 23.) Perspective makes all the difference!

Remember, our liberty is not necessarily permanent. It cannot be taken for granted. Oh, I suppose it can, but it won't last long with such an attitude. It is a gift and a precious one at that. With it, America will endure. Without it, we cannot survive. Great Americans have understood that from the days of the Declaration of Independence and the Constitutional Convention, through two world wars, several "police actions," and down to the present.

There is a price to be paid for liberty. We all owe something to this country. You and I must pay our share of the cost. In one way or another, we must take care of our debt. In fact, unless each one of us Americans understands that great principle and does something about it, we will never be safe.

William Scott was one who paid his debt—almost to the ultimate price. He was a twenty-two-year-old soldier in the Union army. William had spent twenty-four hours on guard duty. Then, unexpectedly, he had to replace one of his buddies who was sick. Forty-eight hours of guard duty without sleep. The inevitable happened, and Scott fell asleep at his post. He was sentenced as a traitor to die by a firing squad.

As the captain heard the judge pronounce sentence on the young soldier, he stepped forward and pled with the judge. "If anyone ought to be shot," he said, "then I should be the one. Please save William's life."

The sorrow and concern of the captain and the other men of William's regiment for their comrade's life touched the heart of the judge. He thought about the matter for a few minutes, and then he turned to the captain and said softly, "There is only one man who can save your friend. Come, we will go to President Lincoln."

A short time later the judge and captain arrived at the White House. Although the president was very busy, he took time to listen quietly to the story the two men told. When they finished, he said, "It would be a sad thing for a young man like William Scott to die like this. I will look into the matter myself this very day."

That afternoon the president went to the guard-house of the army camp. He talked with William about his friends back home, his school, and especially about his mother.

"William, you should be thankful that your mother still lives," President Lincoln said gently. "If I were in your place, I would try to make her a proud mother and never cause her any sorrow."

William listened and then he asked the president a question that had been troubling him. "Would it be possible not to appoint any men from my own regiment to the firing squad?" he asked. "The hardest thing of all would be to die by the hands of my friends."

"My boy," said President Lincoln, "you are not going to be shot tomorrow. I am going to trust you to go back to your regiment. Your country has great need of men like you."

For a moment William could not believe what he had heard. "How can I ever repay you, sir?"

President Lincoln put his hands on the young boy's

shoulders. "My boy," he said, "my bill is a very large one. No money can pay it and no friends can help you. There is only one person in all the world who can pay your debt, and his name is William Scott. If you will fight bravely and do your duty as a soldier, then the debt will be paid. Will you make that promise?"

Well, I probably don't need to tell you that William Scott did both. He made the commitment and he kept it.

I repeat, there is a price for liberty. How are you and I doing?

Liberty is wonderful! I have a firm conviction that it's what we're all about in this country, and if we're going to keep it, you and I must pay our share. In my many travels it is becoming ever more clear to me that more of us must be doing something about that great blessing of liberty.

I ran across an entertaining but perceptive little gem about the importance of "now." It's entitled "On Examining an Inheritance."

> I find a wealth of varied goods
> Enshrouded in protective hoods;
> Preserved, pristine, unscratched, unspent,
> And free from rip or crack or dent.
>
> Aunt's safety box is crammed jamfull
> Of gems wrapped in cotton-wool;
> Expensive scents, unstoppered, stand
> Untouched by frugal soap-sweet land.
>
> She saved her sterling set "for best,"
> (No piece has ever left its nest),
> And ate her meals off earthenware
> (To Staffordshire I now fall heir).

At every turn I find new clues
To things she thought "too nice to use":
Time-weakened silks she never wore;
Expensive rugs she paid to store.

For every joy she tucked away
Against a "very special day,"
Which never dawned, and so to me
Was left this costly potpourri.

The lesson of her life is worth
Much more than all she left on earth.
I've learned it's wise to look ahead,
But wait too long, and friend, you're dead!
(Phyllis I. Rosenteur)

My friends, let's not wait until it's too late. The scenes I described in the beginning are the ones I want for my great-great-grandchildren. But it's up to you and me. We can do it! We can start becoming more aware of the liberties we often take for granted. We can approve all the laws of the land (even the speed limits). We can vote. We can speak up against injustice when we see it. We can pray for those who are elected to lead this country. Above all, we can become educated about what is and is not going on that affects our liberty; and we can pay the price to sustain the good and change the bad. The list is long.

Now, finally, as one who has seen some of this earth's great young men lay down their lives for our freedom, may I add my own voice of gratitude for that liberty. I love this nation and what it represents. Patrick Henry said, "Give me liberty or give me death." May we not have to choose between them. But may God awaken us to choose liberty, whatever the price.

" Next to the bestowal of life itself, the right to direct that life is God's greatest gift to man. Among the immediate obligations and duties resting upon us and one of the most urgent and pressing for attention and action of all liberty-loving people is the preservation of individual liberty. Freedom of choice is more to be treasured than any possession earth can give. It is inherent in the spirit of man. It is a divine gift to every normal being. Whether born in abject poverty or shackled at birth by inherited riches, everyone has this most precious of all life's endowments—the gift of free agency, man's inherited and invaluable right.
Free agency is the impelling source of the soul's progress. It is the purpose of the Lord that man becomes like him. In order for man to achieve this it is necessary for the creator to make him free. "

DAVID O. MCKAY

CHAPTER 17

FREEDOM AND
FREE AGENCY

Anciently the Prophet Joshua, who had on many occasions personally witnessed the great power of the Lord, gave this great and familiar challenge to Israel. "Choose ye this day whom ye will serve." He told them that their choice was to serve the gods of the Amorites or the God of the great patriarchs who lived before the time of the flood. Then he declared with a sureness that was totally consistent with the life he had led, "As for me and my house, we will serve the Lord."

That was a great dilemma for Israel, whether to worship the God of Israel or the more tangible stone gods that sat upon the hillsides or in the Israelites' tents and that were worshipped by pagan neighbors. And all too often they turned from the truth. Why do people do that? Why do they ignore all the witnesses of their own logic as well as the prompting of the Spirit within themselves and turn to such obvious evil as worshipping an idol?

Can the evil one, who has so openly stated his objectives, convince anyone, anyone at all, to join him? Note what the scriptures reveal about his goals and our opportunity to join or reject him.

"Wherefore, men are free according to the flesh; and all things are given them which are expedient unto man. And they are free to choose liberty and eternal life, through the great Mediator of all men, or to choose captivity and death, according to the captivity and power of the devil; for he seeketh that all men might be miserable like unto himself." (2 Nephi 2:27.)

And what excuse will we have? "I don't know" or "the devil was smarter than I" or "the devil made me do it"? Not so! When we turn away from the living God, we do so of our own free will and choice. And when we turn to Him we will find Him there.

But what of those who choose to do evil? And what of those who try to expose evil? Let me share with you a story from the writings of Taylor Caldwell. It takes place in Scotland. Though it is obviously only a legend, it has a most interesting message.

"It seems that centuries ago the devil was incarcerated in the [jail] of an obscure Highland village, charged with various crimes against humanity. No 'advocate' would at first defend him, but a scrupulous judge finally appointed a lawyer for the defense. The entire hamlet was determined that the devil be condemned, including the advocate who was a very religious man of great probity. He spent many nights in desperate prayer. How could he, while maintaining his integrity as the appointed defender of the devil, so present the case to the jury that the devil would be condemned?

"While 'defending' the devil he must also awaken the people to the presence of evil, and its horrors, which the devil represented. He finally hit upon a solution.

"He would reveal the devil in all his power and his terribleness and his infamy while ostensibly defending him! He would gain the admiration of his just neighbors by an open defense, and their respect when he 'lost' the case. Moreover, they would learn to recognize evil forevermore when it was exposed before all eyes.

"So, in court, he conducted the defense brilliantly. He subtly revealed to the judge and the jury and the assembled people all the potency and frightfulness of the devil, by questioning the devil and having him condemn himself by his own words. He adroitly brought out the fact to the people that the devil would not be in their midst without their own guilt and the secret envies, sins and errors in their own hearts. He was able to lead the devil to admit that his plot against mankind had no limits, and, at intervals, the advocate would exhort the people to 'admire' such vast intelligence and wickedness. Stimulated by the advocate's eloquence and apparent defense of him, the devil became even more excessive in his expressed hatred for the world and all in it.

"The people listened with dread and guilt and fear. They remembered their sufferings under the influence of evil, and how they had contributed to the power of that evil, by way of their stupidity and their jealousy of their neighbors, and their avarice and lack of compassion.

"Then the judge charged the jury. He said: 'Evil is among us because we have invited that evil. We have suffered much, but we brought upon our own sufferings. The devil would have had no power over us except that we gave him the power. We became bondsmen because we willed it; we are in despair because we brought despair to our neighbors. We died because we acquiesced in death. We were silent when we should have spoken in behalf of our brothers. For a moment's security we looked away when our neighbor was robbed. In behalf of a false peace we postponed a war with evil when we should not have been moved from our places. At every step we compromised, when we knew there is no compromise with hell. If the devil is guilty, we are not guiltless. In his condemnation, we are included. In a judgment against him we are also judged. May God have mercy on our souls.'

"The devil was condemned to eternal banishment from the hamlet. However, the 'advocate,' in his zeal to expose the devil, had not reckoned with the obtuseness and stupidity of his fellow citizens. They had not understood his plan at all. On the day the devil was banished the 'advocate' was hanged." (*The Devil's Advocate* [New York: MacFadden-Bartell Corp., 1952], pp. 7–8.)

The fate of the advocate and all the people of that village brings to my mind another warning from an ancient prophet. "And thus we see the end of him who perverteth the ways of the Lord; and thus we see that the devil will not support his children at the last day, but doth speedily drag them down to hell" (Alma 30:60).

Now each of us must ask himself a question. And with our life, we will each answer it. Whom will we serve? The true and living God or some idol?

And lest you misunderstand the nature of the true God, let me remind you once more from the scriptures:

"And the arm of the Lord shall be revealed; and the day cometh that they who will not hear the voice of the Lord, neither the voice of his servants, neither give heed to the words of the prophets and apostles, shall be cut off from among the people;

"For they have strayed from mine ordinances, and have broken mine everlasting covenant;

"They seek not the Lord to establish his righteousness, but every man walketh in his own way, and after the image of his own god, whose image is in the likeness of the world, and whose substance is that of an idol." (D&C 1:14–16.)

Each of us stands at the crossroads of good and evil every moment of our lives. And each of us must choose whether he will follow the God Who loves us and desires above all things for us to return to Him, or turn to the image of his own god—and that image is as much an idol as ever an idol was.

Imagine with me, if you will, the sound of a heavy steel door clanging shut, with its clicking sound reverberating loudly. Then the medium-slow sound of footsteps. After a few steps they stop. A key is heard in another steel door and then it swings open, the footsteps begin again as they proceed a short way, the second door clangs shut with deep loud reverberations. The steps continue and fade into the distance.

And so another person walks from the sunlight of freedom into the darkness of prison. Why? Why would a person so live that he gives up that precious treasure we call freedom? Was that his initial intent, that he would do things that would lead him inevitably away from freedom? Was it just chance that he ended up in bondage? Just whose doing was this bondage and how did it all come about?

> Know this that every soul is free,
> To choose his life and what he'll be,
> For this eternal truth is given
> That God will force no man to heav'n.

These words of William C. Clegg hold a key of knowledge that seems to show the lie of those who would blame their troubles onto others. Every person has his share of misfortune, but on the other hand, each of us is given an adequate amount of opportunity.

So often people think of freedom as the opportunity to do whatever they want as long as it doesn't infringe on other people. Such reasoning is nonsense for two reasons: first, everything we do affects, in one way or another, someone else; and second, freedom is not the right to go about doing whatever we want. That is not freedom at all.

Freedom is simple to define, as is usually the case with all true principles. You see, freedom of man, or agency as it is sometimes called, is the right to do right things. No one has the right to do wrong things. A right means that one can do the thing without negative consequences. Our friend who just walked into prison would still be free if he had only acted within the range of activities that were rightfully his to do. But he moved beyond the continuum of his rights into another territory, even to the point where he took advantage of his opportunity to do wrong things. No man has the right to do wrong things, but he does have the opportunity.

And so as we exercise this right to do right, or this opportunity to do wrong, we shape for ourselves a life of freedom or bondage.

The scriptures record, "And now remember, . . . that whosoever perisheth, perisheth unto himself; and whosoever doeth iniquity, doeth it unto himself; for behold, ye are free; ye are permitted to act for yourselves; for behold, God hath given unto you a knowledge and he hath made you free" (Helaman 14:30).

It was not the judge or the jury, nor the arresting officer or the cooperating citizen who sentenced this person to prison. They assisted in his capture and they facilitated the laws of justice as they worked their deeds of keeping peace. But ultimately it was the man who sealed his own fate.

The poet has said:

> All the water in the world,
> However hard it tried,
> Could never sink the smallest ship,
> Unless it gets inside.
> All the evil in the world,
> The blackest kind of sin,
> Can never hurt you one least bit,
> Unless you let it in.

You are the one who will decide what you will think. You are the one who will decide what you will do. And therefore you are finally the one who will decide your own fate or future.

Remember, there is a difference between free will and free agency. Free will is our opportunity to think what we will think. It does not become agency until we act upon it!

Victor E. Frankl, in his enlightening book *Man's Search for Meaning,* was recounting his experiences as a Jew with other Jews in the German concentration camps during the Second World War. He described what began happening to the prisoners:

"I mentioned earlier how everything that was not connected with the immediate task of keeping oneself and one's closest friends alive lost its value. Everything was sacrificed to this end. A man's character became involved to the point that he was caught in a mental turmoil which threatened all the values he held and threw them into doubt. Under the influence of a world which no longer recognized the value of human life and human dignity, which had robbed man of his will and had made him an object to be exterminated (having planned, however, to make full use of him first —to the last ounce of his physical resources)—under this influence the personal ego finally suffered a loss of values."

He goes on to explain in great detail the battle within to retain one's set of values and how person after person surrendered his will and agency and became the animal that the Nazis wanted him to become.

But then he comes to and shares with us some interesting conclusions which he learned under these most difficult conditions. Listen to his words:

"But what about human liberty? Is there no spiritual freedom in regard to behavior and reaction to any given surrounding? Is that theory true which would have us believe that man is no more than a product of many conditional and environmental factors—be they of a biological, psychological or sociological nature? Is man but an accidental product of these? Most important, do the prisoners' reactions to the singular world of the concentration camp prove that man cannot escape the influences of his surroundings? Does man have no choice of action in the face of such circumstances?

"We can answer these questions from experience as well as on principle. The experiences of camp life show that man does have a choice of action. There were enough examples, often of a heroic nature, which proved that apathy could be overcome, irritability suppressed. Man *can* preserve a vestige of spiritual freedom, of independence of mind, even in such terrible conditions of psychic and physical stress.

"We who lived in concentration camps can remember the men who walked through the huts comforting others, giving away their last piece of bread. They may have been few in number, but they offer sufficient proof that everything can be taken from a man but one thing: the last of the human freedoms—to choose one's attitude in any given set of circumstances, to choose one's own way." (From Victor E. Frankl, *Man's Search for Meaning* [Beacon Press, 1958], pp. 78–79, 103–4.)

There are prisons built with dreary walls, the barred windows designed to bid the people who have chosen to give up their freedom by their own disobedience. But there are greater prisons which shackle the mind and those that stifle and eventually smother the spirit. And thus man becomes as imprisoned as if he were shut up eternally in outer darkness. And in fact, that is exactly where he is.

But all this need not be. For man can free himself. He is an agent unto himself to make of himself an individual, a person, a self-actualized being not unlike the angels.

So, if you have pondered the question, "Who am I?" and you feel you do not yet know the answer, you can consider yourself incredibly fortunate. It's true, we do not know. It has not been given or predestined. Rather, we determine it. The blessing of not knowing, and thus being able to determine what we are, is called free agency. Do not misunderstand—we do know that we are children of a loving Heavenly Father, and we know why we are—but what kinds of persons we are and what we will become are ours to decide, and that agency will be the root of our eternal reward or our eternal regret. The choice is ours. Think about it. Think most carefully about it.

❝ As an eighteen-year-old soldier I left the security of parents, the comforts of home, the bounties of life, and the goodness of a blessed land to defend the freedoms of America. In doing so, I saw the reality of hell, the ravages of war, the suffering, pain and death of the innocent, the devastation of homes and lands, and yet, if necessary, and called upon, I would do it again! ❞

PAUL H. DUNN

CHAPTER 18

THE LIGHT
OF LIBERTY

During three years of infantry experience in World War II, I proudly wore a military identification patch on my left shoulder. That patch was an emblem of the Statue of Liberty. The motto of my infantry division was *I'm Proud To Belong,* and that I was! More important, however, I learned from that awful war what the statue really symbolized.

In 1986 we celebrated the one hundredth anniversary of Miss Liberty and enjoyed the marvelous spirit of patriotism that surrounded it. But somehow I had the feeling that many of our citizens, particularly the younger ones, did not fully understand what the statue and America stand for. It's sad but sometimes when we are generations removed from a historical event, we tend to take many things for granted. Could that mean we take America for granted, too? Because that might be so, I was pleased that such emphasis was given to the restoration of the Statue of Liberty. I think that it has made all of us more aware of the values that this national treasure represents.

A hundred years ago when the Statue of Liberty was unveiled for the first time, she stood only for an ideal. Today we not only honor that original ideal but we also honor the many who have sacrificed for it through hard work, defense of our country, and even death in order to turn that ideal into a reality. A hundred years ago Miss Liberty was honored for the promises she made. Today we honor her for the many promises she has kept.

An Armenian immigrant, George Mardikian, tells in his autobiography, *Song of America,* of his very first impressions and experiences as an eighteen-year-old on his first day in America. Walking through an amusement park, he was rather shocked to find grown men and women laughing, singing, behaving like children. He couldn't imagine such frivolous people who seemed unaware that the world was full of suffering and tragedy. But early the next morning he awoke to walk the streets of this disappointing place. He passed a street cleaner sweeping the gutter, and he heard the man humming a happy tune. This fellow with a lowly job—what did he have to sing about? Two big policemen sauntered down the street, and as they passed they gave a young boy a cheery good morning. Gendarmes who smiled and spoke to a total stranger!

Men in work clothes, carrying lunch pails, came from the houses and gathered in friendly groups on the street corners. He heard the clopping of hoofs, and, turning, he saw a milkman deposit bottles on a door-step, then leave. *Precious milk! Won't somebody steal it?* he wondered silently. Later, he told his family, "You know something? They're not crazy, these Americans. *We* are the crazy ones, we people in Europe who go on feeling sorry for ourselves. I want to be an American—another happy, hard-working American!" (*Song of America* [New York: McGraw Hill Book Co., 1956], pp. 50–54.)

Leo Rosten recalls that as a tiny lad, he had the experience of coming to America on an old Dutch immigrant ship with his mother. He remembers:

"The excited throng . . . shouting, 'America! America!'

"Some of the people were laughing, some weeping. And then, through the biting cold and drifting fog of twilight, I beheld an absolutely astonishing sight: a simply enormous statue, higher than the highest hill I had ever seen in my native Poland, a colossus, immense and resplendent, holding high a torch in her great right hand, while her left arm, bent at the elbow, was cradling some object. A box? No, a book—a torch and a book held by this towering edifice which I had been told was the gateway to freedom, the portal to paradise itself. In my confusion (I was not yet four) I wondered, 'Who is that—giant? Why the torch? Why the book?'

"It would be many, many years before I found the answers. And they came not all at once but through the slow accumulation of everyday events—reported remarks of judges, opinions in editorials, arguments in a debate, verdicts forged in crucibles or uncertainty, prejudice and fear—and resolved by the majestic power of reason. The torch, I concluded, was the light of liberty, beckoning all who had left their homes for the dream of being safe and free. The book was the book of laws, the stated, sublime promises that those who came to this land, whatever their name or situation or accent, whatever their origin or poverty or creed, would be protected by that most magnificent of all human conceptions: a government not of kings or caliphs or princes, not of anointed high priests or swaggering sultans, not of those who claimed 'royal blood' or invoked 'divine right'—but a government of commoners bound by inviolable, all embracing laws.''

I am reminded of the experience of the Greek grandmother whose life's dream was to one day become an American citizen:

'' 'Be sure to treat her to dinner before her flight west,' Mother had written from Oregon. But Grandma, as we called her, had other plans. No sooner had the customs man inspected her modest valise than she turned to me, smiling, 'Now, I'll see the Statue of Liberty,' she said.

'' 'But your dinner . . .'

''Grandma's wrinkled chin sharpened between the folds of her black shawl. She stood her ground. 'Food can wait. Liberty cannot.'

''So I changed her ticket and wired home, then hustled her through the city and onto the ferry toward Bedloe [Ellis] Island. Grandmother never flinched. But when we stood looking up at the statue, her peppery eyes turned moist.

'' 'Lee,' she said. Tears flowed down the old face, and her rolling village dialect made the words ring. 'Liberty! Oh, my liberty!'

"I waited before I said, 'Maybe we ought to go inside.'

" 'Inside? And for what?' she asked. 'Inside we see nothing.' Her anger lashed out unexpectedly. Then she smiled again. 'Out here we see liberty.'

" 'Would you like a picture of it?'

"Her face was strong, as proud as the statue's own, yet very much alive. 'Liberty doesn't live on paper. Only in a heart. Do you understand?'

"When I finally led her away, she turned to look back once more. 'Lee,' she said, but to the statue and not to me, 'thank you! Thank you!' "

Over the years America has had its critics—many from without; some from within. Even as laws and men are imperfect, so America has its shortcomings. My father once said: "If there is something wrong in a country—a government, an institution and organization—there are two things you can do: (1) criticize—tear it down, or (2) become a vital part of the system and help change it for the better."

The Lord has said that "governments were instituted of God for the benefit of man, and that he holds men accountable for their acts in relation to them, both in making laws and administering them, for the good and safety of society."

To me America is the greatest country and government on earth. I firmly believe its principles are inspired of God. As columnist Dan Valentine once wrote:

"*America is many things* . . . it's a mood . . . a state of mind . . . a philosophy . . .

"*America is*—a brisk wind from the Atlantic Ocean . . . a soft breeze from the Pacific . . .

"*America* is a mountain peak in Colorado . . . the Mississippi River . . . a snow storm in Montana . . . the hot July sun on the wheatfields of Kansas . . .

"*America* is a small town—with one street light.

"*America* is a big town—with concrete canyons of skyscrapers.

"*America* has broad shoulders . . . and a cocky grin . . . and nervous feet that want to keep moving.

"*America* is restless. It moves . . . it churns . . . it was born in rebellion.

"*America* thrives on hope. It's a second-chance nation—where every man has the right to dream a new dream.

"*America* is the place where losers can become winners . . . where the poor can become rich . . . where the ignorant can become educated . . . where the ill can become healthy . . . where the lost can be found.

"*America* is laughter . . . the hearty grin of a man building a bridge, the giggle of a schoolgirl . . . the happy shouts of boys at play.

"*America* is music . . . the hoe-down fiddle at a country dance, a great symphony playing in a giant hall . . . the Yankee-Doodle turn of a New England town band on the Fourth of July . . .

"*America* is many things: the right to attend church, the right not to attend church . . . the right to speak up, the right to keep quiet . . . the right to join the crowd, the right to walk alone. . . . The ghosts of giant heroes walk the halls of *America's* memory: Patrick Henry . . . Davy Crockett . . . Nathan Hale . . . John Paul Jones . . . Ben Franklin . . . and Washington . . . and Lincoln . . . and Jefferson . . .

"*America* is Thomas Edison . . . and Walt Whitman . . . and Charles Lindbergh . . . and Babe Ruth . . . and Bing Crosby . . . and Willie Mays.

"*America* is the *Mayflower* . . . the Boston Tea Party . . . Bunker Hill . . . Valley Forge . . . Gettysburg . . . The Alamo . . . the Battle of the Marne . . . Guadalcanal, Okinawa . . . Omaha Beach . . . [and Da Nang].

"*America* is a magic mixture of all the people of the world . . . English, Scots, and Germans pushing back the wilderness . . . Italians, Dutch, and Swedes walking across the plains to a new tomorrow . . . Jews, Poles, and the French blending together to make a dream come true . . . People of all races and creeds working together to create a nation . . .

"*America* is many things . . . the Statue of Liberty . . . Mount Rushmore . . . Freeways . . . Yankee Stadium . . . Yellowstone Park . . .

"*America* is a traffic jam . . . an election day . . . a town meeting . . . a little league baseball game . . . a junior prom . . . a Labor Day parade . . . a trip to the moon . . .

"*America* is the right to work at a job, the right to quit a job . . . the right to own property . . . the right to compete . . . the right to follow a dream . . .

"*America* is many things . . . a mood, a state of mind . . . a philosophy . . .

"*America* is a red, white, and blue tomorrow for all men who hold the hope of freedom in their hearts." (*Spirit of America* [in *American Essays,* no. 9, 1972], p. 1.)

May God always bless America and those of us who have the responsibility to preserve her!

INDEX